UNBREAKABLE RHYTHM

My Journey Through Music, Wellness & Mental Strength

by

FRANK ZUMMO

with Jason Pettigrew

UNBREAKABLE RHYTHM:
My Journey Through Music, Wellness & Mental Strength

Produced by Frank Zummo and Jason Pettigrew

First North American Edition: 2025

The events, locations, and conversations in this book, while true, are recreated from the authors' memory. However, the essence of the story and the feelings and emotions evoked are intended to be accurate representations. In certain instances, names, persons, organizations, and places have been changed to protect an individual's privacy.

ISBN: 9798350169782
Printed and bound in the United States
Executive Producer: David Frangioni
Production Manager: Ricardo Rodriguez
Art Director: Charlie Weinmann
Copy Editor: Ben Davis

Published by Modern Drummer Publications
Modern Drummer
1279 West Palmetto Park Road
Boca Raton, FL 33427
moderndrummer.com

Make Art, no matter how big it is, with beauty and creativity.

I remember Frankie and Christie would be in the backyard... little tent things and bricks and so on... and they would make Art. They would make stories, among themselves. They grew up understanding this kind of beauty... and you can't find that, you can't buy it either. And this is what he has... that's what you have. You share some commonality with both of you. The beauty of a noise, a singing, a sound. This is what makes life love: Art. The art he creates with a drumstick and a metal piece and so forth, that's Art and Beauty and Love.

Make it Art. Make it work. Use your imagination. *Make* it work. Don't settle for shit.

Frederic "Poppa" DeFeis

1926–2018

This was the speech my Poppa gave at my wedding rehearsal dinner that brought down the house. I felt this was the perfect way to kick off this book and honor his legacy. — FZ

CONTENTS

FOREWORD

In the mid 2000s I found myself at a crossroads with my band, thenewno2. We'd recorded an album, played Coachella and Lollapalooza, done a residency at The Key Club on the Sunset Strip, and performed as musical guests on *The Late Show with Conan O'Brien*. Then my best friend, writing partner and drummer, decided to change his creative path and leave music altogether. I was very sad, and scared that this might mean the end of the band we had moved to Los Angeles to form and both worked so hard for since my father's passing in 2001. Thankfully, the remaining band members were incredibly supportive, and refused to let me give up. They lovingly pushed me to record a second album, *thefearofmissingout*. So we began the search for someone who might share our musical sensibility enough to fill the empty seat.

This led us surprisingly rapidly to Frank, whose group Street Drum Corps ran in similar friendship circles. His love for electronic music and rock, and his deep love for the Bristol sound, made him the perfect choice for what we were preparing to record. At the time, we had no idea how much Frank was to elevate us, both musically and energetically, but we soon found out during what became affectionately known as the "Fisher-Price: My First Tour," a brilliantly naive romp through some of the more squalid clubs in the United States. Though it did include one of the most magical nights of my life, spent in what Frank referred to as "Imagination Land."

Instantly, Frank became the heart of the band. There is a subtle yet extremely powerful aura to the man, which, I admit, was completely lost on me the first time I met him and saw his signature look of tattoos, tight vest, and mohawk. But once I had locked eyes with him a few times (as you do with your drummer when things onstage are going in one direction or the other), I saw, beneath this mixture of precision and strength, a kind-eyed, fiercely disciplined monk of a soul staring back at me. Completely in command of his power and emotion, like some musical variant of a Shaolin master, lifting his sticks, with straight arms, directly to the sky (in the manner that Thor would wield Mjölnir) and bringing them thundering down onto the skins. I thought this summoning of magical energy might be a one-off thing during the finale of our set and that it would prove too exhausting to maintain for any great length of time. Yet here we are 20 years later, and it still looks wonderfully exhausting. Exhausting, and fun.

Consistency like this can't be cultivated—it comes from deep down in Frank's core. He's one of the hardest-working people I have ever met, both on and off the stage. He's always striving to create human connections and build community, and we see this in everything he does. Whether it's playing live, recording, or mentoring younger musicians, Frank gives 150 percent across the board. He doesn't just show up and play, he invests himself fully, making sure the people around him feel supported and inspired. That level of commitment to kindness and perfection is extremely rare, and it's what makes him such a powerful force, both as a drummer and as a human being. To watch Frank play is to witness someone pour their soul into every beat, and that's what Frank has done for his whole life as a drummer. This is what he does for the people he chooses to play with, every night, wherever the music takes him. Frank is a rhythmical monster, with the heart of a lion and the gentle, kind manners that endear him to every band-mum he has broken bread with on his travels.

Though our time playing together was brief, Frank has become a lifelong brother of mine. He even persuaded me to become ordained as a Minister in the state of California so I could conduct the wedding ceremony between him and his dear wife Lauren, the mother of his two wonderful sons Brixton and Riot, to whom I am godfather. This was a task that was as stressful as it was mind-expanding, and to this date, I have presided over the ceremonies of many other dear friends in a myriad of different countries, probably illegally, although I've never mentioned this to them.

Bravo, Frank! I love you, and thank you for your love and rhythm all these years.

I can neither confirm nor deny any of the stories in this book.

Dhani Harrison
FPSHOT 2025

With Jason Pettigrew at School of Rock Workshop at House of Vans Chicago.
Here is where this book was born and the introduction of this book was written (2023).

INTRODUCTION

A lot of musicians write books to share their stories, from their creative lives to their crazy tour tales to more scandalous moments. This is not that book.

From the beginning, my mission has been seeing how these workshop events were saving lives firsthand, motivating and inspiring people. I do five to seven events a year—a small number compared to the sheer size of the world. I want this message to be heard around the world, and that's why this is in a book: because I can't be everywhere I want to be. The goal is to put what I do—and the message—into a book to inspire people, motivate them, and supply them with the resources to get help. And then take all this and intertwine it, obviously, with stories of what I've experienced.

The kids at these events see pictures of me at these giant festivals in front of thousands of people and on TV, and they just think I'm a superhero. I'm no different from any of these kids: I just had a vision and a path, and I stayed on it until it happened. That's what I'm preaching out here. There's no reason why they can't be up here if they stay on that same path. So, if I can relay that message and intertwine all the amazing things that got me to this place, my hope is it will help instill people with some much-needed joy. I've been so fortunate to have this life and these experiences. And as a young kid who came from nothing, it's just crazy.

There's this great book called *The Art of Fear* by Kristen Ulmer. She was the world's most extreme female skier at a time when girls were not doing that, and she was surpassing the guy skiers. It's a really well-done book that talks about fear and her relationship with it, and I got into it because I was having some issues with that subject. I'll tell the kids who come to the events something about "having fun with fear tonight," because it's something that people simply don't do. They *think* about fear, and we're always being told "don't be afraid" or "no fear." And it's like, *no*. Shit is scary, and Ulmer's book talks about that, but it's also interwoven with all her great stories and experiences. It's not just a "look at me and all the rad shit I've done" book: I found it both very empowering and necessary. I've never skied in my life (and I never will), but that book is *incredible*. It didn't matter that I wasn't a skier: The whole point of this book should be that if you're not a drummer or any kind of musician, you should still feel triumphant when you're done reading it. You should be left feeling inspired and fired up—we need more of that in this world! There's just too much dark, negative bullshit.

I wish so many more people who have way more visibility than me would use their forums for good. Most band dudes post to their social media platforms about how rad their life is. You know, posting pictures of their famous wives or with celebrities. What does that show the kids? Showing a kid that, "Oh, if you're a rock star, you have to date a famous girl and post pictures of her ass in a bikini." *That's not what it's about.* The people that I look up to use their platforms to give back, motivate, and inspire. Because to me, that's what being a true artist—and even just a *human*—is about.

But right now, it's the day before the final Sum 41 performance at the Juno Awards, where we'll close the show with our last-ever performance and then get inducted into the Canadian Music Hall of Fame. My fear and anxiety are set to "stun." It's over tomorrow, and the reality of what's next is here!

More on that later...

1
THE BEGINNING

I was born on July 2, 1978, in West Islip, New York, the son of Frank and Danae DeFeis Zummo. I had a pretty great childhood, but I can tell you I have three top childhood memories that really stand out. Some semi-important details have been lost to time, but I do have three distinct memories.

Actually, I needed my mom to help me out with the first one. I did one of my workshops in Toronto in between the last two Sum 41 shows on the final tour in 2025. Somebody asked me when I first became interested in drums. I said, "Actually, I haven't really known. I've been giving a rough estimate, you know, like a couple years old. But my mom's here, let's ask her. Mom: How old was I when I left the kitchen table and the next thing you and Dad heard was me playing drums?" She immediately replied, "Two."

My dad had his drums set up in one of the bedrooms of the little apartment where I lived for the first couple of years of my life. I just went into that room and started playing. Now normally, kids pick up sticks and it's just an all-over-the-place racket. But my parents said they could tell the first time I was hitting those drums at two years old that there was something special there. It didn't sound like a two-year-old just hitting drums for the first time. Thanks, Mom!

My second earliest memory ignited my future, inspired my career, and continues to fire my heart up. In January 1984, my parents took me to see Mötley Crüe co-headlining with Ozzy Osbourne at the Nassau Coliseum. I was five years old. The three of us were in the total nosebleed section, and I was completely in awe of Mötley Crüe—especially Tommy Lee. That was the day I decided that all I wanted to do in life was to play the drums. Everything I have learned, worked through, and engaged with in my professional life all stems from this show. (Quick foreshadowing: When people tell you that "you should never meet your idols," it's probably because their heroes are shitty. I'm friends with *my* idol.)

The shit I was into was definitely metal: Ozzy and Mötley Crüe and stuff like that. But my introduction to music was my dad's record collection. He was a radio DJ in college, and I still have his records to this day. It was all the biggest groove records of all time: Led Zeppelin, Sly and the Family Stone, James Brown, George Clinton. Funk and rock—that was my foundation. That's why I'm such a groove-oriented drummer compared to that Neil Peart style of technical drumming. My dad gave me his record collection and a set of headphones and just said, "Have at it." So I had self-discovery until I was six, and then I got formal lessons from six to my so-called "college years."

I literally still have the tapes right here in my studio: I found them in my Mom's attic. I've got *Led Zeppelin IV*, the one with "Black Dog" and "Rock and Roll" on it, which were two songs I would just play over and over again. Mötley Crüe's *Shout at the Devil* and *Theatre of Pain*. Metallica's *Ride the Lightning* and *...And Justice for All*. The live Slayer record, *Decade of Aggression*, and some Anthrax. This was the stuff that I would just, fucking *rock...*

When I was seven years old, the drum school I attended held this "Battle of the Beats" drum competition where everyone had to go solo for maybe two, three minutes max. The event was at Hofstra University in Long Island in this massive, beautiful theater. I had the big double-bass, rock 'n' roll drum set. You could barely see me behind the kit. I was in the first category and was the youngest in the grouping. I purposely started with a basic rock beat, and then flipped it into the most insane double-bass solo for the duration—just no mercy the whole time—and the whole audience erupted into wild applause. (I had the VHS tape of this digitized in the last couple of years and it's on my YouTube channel now.) I won first place. The prize was a beautiful Ludwig maple drum set. That really kicked things off for me in a big way. I went back and competed years later when you got to actually play with a band onstage. I was sick as a dog—and I won again! I never competed or did anything like that again until the AltPress awards show in 2017 when I won in the Best Drummer category.

DANAE DEFEIS, school secretary, part-time singer, proud mom:
When I was pregnant with him, I was in a band. So I guess the vibe went into him, because I sang until I was six months pregnant with him. I used to go down and jam with him and his friends. I used to yell down, "Hey guys! You want to jam?" Usually some Janis Joplin. So I would jam with him. The neighbors would complain about the drumming. They'd come over and say it was too loud, and I'd say, "He's inside!" and close the door on them, unapologetic.

The third earliest memory I had was being three and going to the hospital to see my little sister, Christie. I didn't get to hold her or anything because this was in the old days: I had to look at her through a glass window in the maternity ward. My dad pointed her out to me and said, "That's your sister," and then took me home. I couldn't see my mom, either: I wasn't allowed to go in her room. I will remember this much later on when my beautiful wife gives birth to our first son.

CHRISTIE POIRIER, Frank's sister:
Frank is three years older than me. I can't remember him *not* playing the drums. In our family, we're all performing artists, so I never thought much about it—it's just what he did. He was always in the basement playing drums. He had his own studio. Sometimes I'd go down there and he'd let me hang out. I'd watch him or something. It was always some kind of performance that we were doing. It was totally normal. And so great.

We were a very strict Italian family. No matter what, our family always had dinner together every night. We weren't sitting in front of the TV—we were *together*. It was always family time. I'd come home from school, and I would go straight to the basement and practice drums. When my mom flashed the basement lights on and off, that meant it was time to come up for dinner.

Every Sunday, we would go to my grandparents' house for a family dinner. That was what we always did. We looked forward to the holidays and everything. That's how I grew up. It's really important to just disconnect and have that family time with everybody. When it was dinnertime or the Sunday family tradition or the holidays, we were always together.

My grandfather, "Poppa DeFeis," was my biggest mentor. Without him, I probably wouldn't have all the skills I have. He was a theater person: he ran his own theater and had me working there as a kid with all these responsibilities. That's where I learned it all because if I didn't do *one* thing, the *whole* thing would fall apart. He had children's shows every weekend. I was the usher, the sound guy, the lighting guy, the costume guy, the prop master—*everything*. I had my checklist, and I better have checked all the boxes off that shit *twice* because I didn't want my grandfather coming down on me. It was a very serious thing. I think that's where I learned my discipline, organizational skills, and sense of responsibility.

POIRIER: Our grandfather owned a theater on Long Island. His was one of the top theaters in the city. Our parents met in a band. I took dance lessons; I was a professional dancer for quite some time. Uncle Dave was in the band Virgin Steele, and we'd see him practice at my grandmother's house in her basement. That was our normal family. Some families like to go to baseball games or do sports stuff; our sports were music, dance, and performing arts with the theater. There was always some kind of performing arts happening.

One year, we were on vacation in Florida. My parents saw that we could sell this little house we had and buy a brand-new big house (with land!) in Florida. I didn't want to go: I didn't want to leave my friends. It was really hard. We moved and we—my mom, my sister, and I—fucking hated it. The bullying was at another level. No musicians. No music teachers. We were way out in farmland. I was always in trouble. I didn't fit in or didn't know how to navigate situations. Plus, there are no basements in Florida, so I would have to play my drums in our sweltering garage.

Fortunately, we moved back in time for eighth grade, and my parents got a house in Wheatley Heights, New York. Our development was on the borderline of both good and bad neighborhoods. The giant high school was a very fucking snooty, upper-class school. When I got there, it was a lot of posh kids with sports cars doing drugs, fake rebellion wrapped in entitlement posturing.

I wasn't in bands with buddies when I was in elementary school. That was because there weren't many musicians at the level I was at to actually be in a band with me. Because I started playing so early and was at such a pro level at such a young age, it was hard to find competent musicians around my age that I could be in bands with. So I would just go home and play my tapes because that's all I had—which was fine. I had my drums set up; I had lighting in my basement. It was a vibe, and I felt like I was in those bands whose music I practiced along with.

When I finally got to high school, things changed. I was at the Sam Ash Music store and saw the bulletin board where players would post fliers with those little tags you pull off with a phone number on them. There was this virtuoso guitar player kid who had a flier that caught my eye. I had a bass player friend who was also amazingly talented. We were in one of those prog bands (not like Rush, more like Living Colour), flashy players with tons of fireworks and all that. Those two guys and I would get in my basement every fucking day and just shred and write all these crazy instrumental songs. I went from being alone and playing to my records to jamming with these amazing virtuoso players and playing all this really hard shit. We were playing metal, funk, and rock—and whatever the fuck we wanted. Woodshedding was such a great foundation for me, finally allowing me to play with some insane players and learn all that stuff.

We didn't have a name, and we never gigged out. It was just a band where we would jam after school and on weekends. It was me, a bass player, and a guitar player. Everybody was just playing a lot of notes, but there was a ton of feel and style. These guys were both such amazing musicians. And then what wound up happening was the bass player and I turned that into one of my first hardcore bands, Planet Freek. Basically, Planet Freek came out of this wild, muso mindset and evolved into this hardcore-punk thing. Then that bass player ended up quitting, and it just became a straight-up hardcore band at that point. I did the hardcore scene for a couple years and then it died anyway because it got too violent.

POIRIER: He got arrested for doing graffiti when he was a teenager. There was a big crackdown in Long Island on graffiti. That was a big part of the New York hardcore scene—that was the thing. It was a big part of it. I think some kids ratted him out and the cops arrested him. Mom got him out and was like, "OK, this was stupid. It's all right, though, we'll get through this." Then the cops actually came to his high school and arrested him again just to make it some public spectacle or something! That was really embarrassing for him. Maybe he doesn't want that in his book, but it was devastating. He never did anything stupid like that again for the rest of his life.

He moved on after that. I think that whole scene was dying anyway. It was a rough scene at the time. I remember going to a show in Huntington. There was like a legit fight, and it was really scary. My brother grabbed me and we ran out. It was the last show he ever played in that scene. It was getting to be too much. Gangs were getting involved and it wasn't even about the music anymore. Shortly afterward, he got gigs in cover bands while he was still a senior in high school.

I was in a big cover band that was playing in the tri-state area. We had a Thursday night residency, and in Brooklyn, the bars are open till 4 in the morning. So we'd play til almost 4 and then have to load out everything. I'd get home at probably 5 in the morning, sleep for an hour or two, and then go to school on Friday. Then after school, I'd go do all that again to play a gig in Manhattan.

I enrolled myself in the Drummers Collective in New York City and studied with an Afro-Cuban teacher and a Broadway show drum teacher, shit that was so far out of my comfort zone. *I'm gonna learn every fucking style. I'm going to learn to read music better. I'm gonna take every gig.* I played on a cruise ship in Alaska; I played in theme parks; I went to audition for *Stomp*: *I just wanted to work as a drummer.* I'm going to become well-rounded so I can always work as a drummer because there is no Plan B. I want to play drums. I'll play in a fucking polka band and still be happy because *I'm playing drums.*

When I went to the Drummers Collective, I was determined to well-round myself as a drummer so I could work forever, no matter what. So I picked two teachers. I think the instructor who was doing Broadway shows played in an orchestra; I could learn that world and get my reading at the level it needed to be. Then I took a class taught by Bobby Sanabria of Afro-Cuban Latin styles. I didn't listen to that kind of music, and it felt like learning another language. With that kind of music, all your limbs are playing different rhythms using different time signatures. It was the hardest thing I've ever had to do. Bobby was hard on me: I would have to go home and practice for the week, then take the train in New York City and walk a whole bunch of blocks. And if I didn't nail what he gave me to practice, he would send me home.

That shit was hard, but learning those rhythms opened up my palette to so much more, especially later on in Street Drum Corps. That stuff just came out organically. I was playing all these crazy Latin/bossa nova rhythms. It's funny because when I was training a lot of the Street Drum Corps players, the parts of the songs the drummers would have issues with were the ones I learned with Bobby Sanabria.

Here's how much I knew that I wanted to play drums for life: when I was in elementary school, I would practice my fucking signature for when I'd have to sign autographs—*because I wanted to*. I just knew I wanted it. Because that was part of being an artist: signing stuff. Because of that, I was motivated to learn cursive writing. So I'm on my way. (You know, being an artist requires that I have a cool signature!) That was so crazy to think about back then. Later on, when I was a bit older and was going from class to class, I'd pull out my Walkman and put my fucking headphones on and listen to my favorite songs as if everything around me was part of a music video. As I was walking through the halls, I remember orchestrating it like it was a music video and I was the star. That's how I got through school, because I didn't enjoy it. I made my own world, and music got me through it. Going from class to class: I'm listening to my favorite cassette tapes. Being on the school bus: I'm listening to my favorite cassette tapes. I just couldn't wait to get home, go into the basement, and pretend I was in Ozzy's band playing a concert.

I started a cover band in high school called Rosetta Stone. The girl who sang in that band, her father owned an entertainment company that provided bands for weddings, lounges, all that. We played a show and her dad came out, saw me, and was like, "This kid is amazing." He put me in his wedding/lounge/cover band called Creation, and that's where I had my first paid gigs. I would go play every weekend. I could play every standard—Italian, Jewish, even fucking Celine Dion—wearing a tuxedo. It was serious. I was so young, just like 15 or 16 years old.

I'm glad I didn't grow up with all this insane social media garbage kids deal with now. I went through that in more of the traditional way when I was coming up. When I was in school, it wasn't cool to be a musician; liking Metallica and having long hair is cool now, but since I wore combat boots and Metallica shirts and had long hair and played drums, I was bullied to the max. I did not have a healthy relationship with school. The kids who liked heavy music were like the dirtbags, the outcasts. I would get on the bus, and gum would get thrown in my hair, which I would have to get cut out when I got to school. I did not have it easy in school—it sucked.

I met with my high school guidance counselor during my senior year. I remember when it was time for students to prepare for college applications and SATs and all that kind of stuff. She actually said to me, "Hey, so you're already doing what you want to be doing. I know you're in a band and I know you're getting home really late. Do you want to get out of here early, so you're not dealing with this insane schedule?"

She said I could double up and do my senior year in half a year. I would have to take all the classes that I would have normally taken in the year, but in half the time. "You'll have to work your ass off, but then when you leave for Christmas break, you'll be done. And then you come back in June and go to graduation and get your diploma." I was like, "Holy shit!" I worked so hard and graduated in the winter, and then I just went on the road and did what I was doing without having to attend any classes. The fact that my guidance counselor acknowledged me in a sea of hundreds of kids was really inspiring and sent me on my way. Bless that lady! I forget her name, but she was amazing. It was great because I didn't like school to begin with, and to be able to get out and then go live my dream and go on the road? It was perfect.

At the time, The Zoo was the biggest cover band in their scene. Their drummer left, I auditioned, and they immediately offered me the gig. They asked me how soon I could jump in and start, and I was like, "Well, I'm not going to my prom, but my best friend is having a graduation party that I want to go to." And they were laughing hysterically because I was so fucking young. I was 17 and had gotten into a huge band that was sponsored by Bud Light. We had a road crew, we had production. The Zoo had won some cover band contests on MTV; I got in the area's biggest band and I was a fucking kid. And it was *awesome*, you know?

I did that for years. That was my boot camp, playing three hours of all this Top 40 music and classics every night. I got to go on the road, too. I'm making great money playing drums and it was so rad; and it was awesome that it literally coincided with my early graduation. Getting an audition was better than getting the gig: I think I got paid $100 a gig, and I thought I was fucking rich because I didn't have any bills. But I had tunnel vision. *Let me get through this. Let me fucking pass. Let me get out of here so I can live my dreams.* I would spend my lunch breaks doing my homework, so when I got home, I'd be done with school and I could be in the basement playing along to my Metallica and Mötley Crüe records, pretending I was in those bands. That's what I wanted to do. I didn't care about anything else.

So when I'm asked how I got to be in Mötley Crüe without an audition, well, it's because *I had been auditioning my whole life for that moment. My entire childhood.* I put on these records from start to finish and played as if I was actually in the band. I'd get dressed up like I was performing in one of their shows and go down there and fucking rock out. I spent my whole life getting ready for this.

I was in an original band called Alien Pop, named after those funky lollipop candies that look like aliens. It was like a blend of Jane's Addiction, Depeche Mode, and dance music. It was fucking *awesome*. We played the New York City circuit and we also did the Winter Music Conference in Miami. That was my first time attending a dance music event, and best of all, we showcased at the Fontainebleau Miami Outdoors. I had drum triggers and pads with cards you had to load and play. I was going to underground house music clubs in NYC. I was fully in that world back when I wasn't even old enough to get into these clubs, you know? Alien Pop was a real original band that was playing shows and recording. And it fell apart because it just wasn't a healthy, happy band.

Dom Famularo was one of the most well-known drum teachers and motivational speakers. He is where I got a lot of my inspiration and techniques. I talked to him right before he passed away from cancer, and I thanked him for everything. I went to him to learn technique, and that was extremely hard; I had to essentially relearn how to hit the drums, because the way I was doing it, he explained, "You're not going to last if you keep hitting the drums the way you're doing it now." He came into my life at a time when I was in my first electronic band, Alien Pop, and I had to play to loops and programmed parts. The band was telling me that I didn't have a good enough pocket and my tempo wasn't right. So I went to Dom, shared their gripes, and he just listened.

We did a bunch of sessions. And then he said to me one day, "Hey dude: Your groove and your tempo are fine—those guys are *wrong*. Keep doing what you're doing." That was great because, before he said that, it was the first time anybody told me that I wasn't good. My whole life, I had been praised as a prodigy drummer, and now I'm in this electronic band playing with machines, and all this shit they're telling me was mentally not healthy. I was, for the first time, insecure behind the drum set. So instead of just feeling defeated, I said, *OK, I'm going to go to all of these different drum teachers and work on this.* We just needed to refine my technique and all that. Dom really motivated and inspired me during a dark time.

Around that same time, Dom sent me to Al Miller, a very famous big band drummer. When I went to him, Dom gave me a note that read, "Hey Al: Meet Frank. Kick his ass reading. Dom." I go to Al's, and he's got this huge big band drumset. He would put on Buddy Rich songs and pull out the charts. You know, that music is fast, and as things are going by, you're flipping pages while you're drumming. My reading really wasn't that good at that point, but this guy, this old-school man just kicked my ass at reading. That was really, *really* hard.

When Alien Pop was falling apart, I was thinking, "Maybe I need to go to college." I applied to Five Towns Music College, which is a prestigious, high-end private music school. My uncle had gone there, and I got in, but I was like, "I can't afford this. My parents are getting divorced. I don't make much money." So I applied for a scholarship, and they actually gave me one. There wasn't an audition; it was more about testing—testing and a lot of meetings.

The day I went there to meet with the person to pick out all my classes, I walked in thinking it was an all-music school. But it had expanded significantly since my uncle went there. There were dormitories now and they had a basketball team. I walked past the basketball team as they were practicing, and it instantly gave me the feelings of when I was in elementary school, which I disliked. I went to the academic advisor and I was like, "I can't do this. Thank you guys for giving me this opportunity. But I can't do this."

DEFEIS: I had no advice for him. I never told him what he could or couldn't do. I said "Do you want to see about going to college for music maybe?" So he got all his expenses paid. All right by us here! Then he went and he said, "Ma, it's not for me." I said, "That's fine." There was no need for him to go to college. He didn't need to, you know? It was more of a learning experience on his own.

Not taking that music school scholarship and instead going to all these independent teachers and The Drummers Collective changed my whole world. Learning all this other stuff they were able to show me just motivated me to become a better drummer. All of this amazing experience I was exposed to built a really important foundation. You may love just punk-rock music, but you know what? Learn Latin music. Learn jazz. Just get well-rounded and learn to expand your palate.

When I took that gig on the cruise ship, we were playing Broadway-style shows, backing comedians, and playing jazz gigs. Playing on a cruise ship was probably the hardest thing I've ever had to do in my life. Every day was a different show, and you literally had just one rehearsal, and then had to play all the material you just learned the very next night. I was 22, had gotten instruction from amazing teachers, and I auditioned for *everything*.

So, I'm going on 22. That summer, after completing all these drum lessons, is when I started auditioning for everything. I was auditioning for any commercial or movie that needed a drummer. I was going to New York City for auditions (I had headshots done!) and all this stuff to just round myself, and to try for anything else I could possibly get.

I went to the venue where my cover band was playing. They let me in there after hours, and I brought a film crew and shot a promo video. I built a backing track of me playing every style of music, performing a drum solo, talking about myself, and I showed some live clips. That was like my little reel. That's when I auditioned for *Stomp*. I got cut right away, though; didn't even make it to the second round. Years later, I auditioned again and made it to the final round: I was going to get hired! And then they closed down their show in Boston and put that cast out on the tour. So they weren't going to hire more people after all. I tried to audition for Blue Man Group but never got the chance.

I took my promo videotape (VHS format!) and sent it to the casting people for Hershey Park, and I got hired the day they called me. They were like, "You sure you want to work at a theme park? This video is very professional, and you're such a skilled musician." I'm like, "Yeah." Hershey Park had a drum show that featured playing on trash called The Trash Time Band. I took that gig. It was a whole summer gig. We worked six days a week playing on trash. It was a dream, fun, summer gig.

I wound up getting hired on Holland America Cruise Lines to go to Alaska and play in the orchestra. I went directly from finishing my Hershey Park contract to flying to Vancouver to hop on a cruise ship and do that gig. I was just doing all of this to build my résumé.

When I got home from the cruise ship, my uncle—whom I had looked up to my whole life—called me. He was the singer of the heavy metal band Virgin Steele, which was quite popular in Europe. I grew up going to all their gigs and watching them rehearse in my grandmother's basement. He said, "You know, I need a drummer. We're doing a huge two-month European arena tour as main support for Hammerfall. Do you want to do this?" And I was like, *Dude, I've been waiting for you to ask me to do this my whole life. Let's fucking go.* So we rehearsed for a month and I went to Europe. That was my first tour. It kind of threw me, because on my first tour, I'm playing arenas; I have a drum tech, tour bus, production, hotels—that's what I thought touring was. I was 22 years old. So I'm in Europe for the first time ever, playing these massive fucking shows.

And then, when I came home and needed to work, The Zoo called me back. So I got back in The Zoo, but that was just a placeholder, something that'd be fine for the time being. I knew I was just doing this to keep working and playing drums. That's when I started forming original bands and doing the whole showcasing thing.

One of the best pieces of advice my grandfather ever gave me was that if you're starting something new, "See it through. And at the end of the year, reassess the growth of it. Are you happy? How far have you come? Is there progress? Are we having things happen? Is there momentum? If not, it's time to reevaluate." That's how I've looked at every project. Things take time, but if we're at the end of the year of this new project and haven't done anything, then it's time to fucking move on. He was just such a father figure and really taught me so much about the business—lessons that I still apply to this day.

I realized it was time to move on. I didn't want to stay with The Zoo and be stuck in the cover scene forever. The original music scene was really fucking hard to break into, but I didn't wanna play in a Broadway orchestra in the pit, under the stage; I wanted to be *on* the stage. I recognized that the window of what I wanted to do wasn't gonna open there, especially when my original band broke up after we had worked so hard.

The guitarist from The Zoo and I started an original band called Red Karma, and that was the first real band I ever had. We had everything in place: management, legal and booking teams, all set to launch. We started doing showcases all over New York City for record labels. And it started to happen: It was the first time an original band of mine was really happening. Except we didn't know that our singer was a heroin addict. I'd never been around a heroin addict, so I didn't know the signs. Our manager said, "I'm stepping down from managing this band because this isn't healthy and your singer needs to get well." The band was done. I was devastated because we had worked so hard to get it there.

But this manager, John Germinario, pulled me aside. "Hey, I just started working with a singer-songwriter. She's French Canadian. She's got a finished record in the can. She just needs to put together a band and prove that they are kickass live, and then they're going to put this record out. She's going to get a record deal. They're going to go on tour. You need to audition for this band."

I auditioned for the band, got the gig, hit it off with them, and went back a couple of weeks later. We did showcases, and we were in the parking lot at that first showcase with our manager when he goes, "You've got to move here, dude. I'm watching the room light up and everybody is looking at you drumming. You need to move here."

And I was like, *done*. I've always wanted to move to California. Everything I love about music is here. I've been coming here for years. Obviously, if you think that I'm sticking out here in a good way, yeah, I'm going to do it.

I immediately called my mom and said I was quitting The Zoo and moving to California. She said, "OK. Come home, I'll help you get ready. What do you need?"

2
CALIFORNIA, MEET ZUMMO!

I had no idea how many "firsts" I'd experience moving to LA. I had no fucking money because I spent it all fixing my damn car. You need a car in LA to go *anywhere*—especially as a drummer. I was living in a shitty, roach-infested apartment in Koreatown. Today, Koreatown is very bougie; it definitely wasn't when I was there. It was the first time I woke up to a roach running across my stomach, and I'm not a filthy person. (I'm a neat freak, actually.)

Before Street Drum Corps took off, I needed to make some money, so I went to Guitar Center and all the drum shops in town, but nobody was hiring. I was trying to get a job *anywhere*. I remember going to this one place, being there 15 minutes early for an interview, and nobody would let me inside the store. I finally had to wave to somebody walking by the entrance to let me in. When I got to the drum department, the staffer lectured me, saying, "If you wanna work here, you need to be on time." And I was like, "Dude, I was here, I couldn't get in the door." And this guy just kept reprimanding me. Did I even *want* to work with people like this?

Right around this time, when I really needed work, The Zoo called me and said they were doing a residency for spring break in Florida. The guy who replaced me was a schoolteacher or something—he didn't have the same spring break: Could I come? I flew out and did the spring break gig with The Zoo, and made enough cash to pay my rent for the month. That was pretty cool, and I got to work with them again.

I auditioned for one of LA's best bands, theStart, who were fiercely DIY. It was my first time on a band trailer tour. No techs. We drove ourselves. We loaded in our gear and merchandise, slept in the van, shared one hotel room, and crashed on friends' floors. I had never done anything like that.

I did a whole tour cycle with them, supporting Goldfinger and playing in House of Blues–sized venues. It was always just America and Canada, we never went overseas. I think theStart is where most people recognized me as a drummer. At the beginning of Street Drum Corps, I wasn't playing a traditional kit, so people in the industry didn't really know my skill on the drums. But theStart was such a cool

LA band: when we would play the Troubadour and The Key Club, it'd be totally fucking sold out and all the cool bands and industry people would be there.

In the middle of my tour cycle with theStart, I don't think Bobby Alt had officially shared Street Drum Corps with Kevin Lyman and the Warped Tour staff yet. Around that time, we did an anti-NAMM gig. NAMM (the National Association of Music Merchandisers) is the musical instrument convention held in Anaheim every January. Every NAMM concert is like a clinic—just every virtuoso jamming with all these other virtuosos. So we went to Anaheim punk HQ Chain Reaction and built a drum show with rock stars—like punk-rock stars. We brought in John Sawicki from *Stomp* to choreograph the whole circus. We had Brooks Wackerman from Bad Religion, Adrian Young from No Doubt, just all these rock stars, and we built this wild show that ended up selling out.

Somehow, Lyman found out about our show. He called Bobby and said, "Come to my house, let's talk about what you're doing. Why do I not know about this?" Bobby goes to his house and they have a meeting. So while I'm touring with theStart, Bobby calls me and goes, "Yo, we just got the Warped Tour. Kevin says he doesn't have a stage for us, but if we can bring our own, he'll put us in a good spot. We gotta find sponsors to rent a van and trailer, bring a stage and sound—and we've got to do it all ourselves."

OK. Challenge accepted. We had something like 10 sponsors. Some gave us 10 bucks. One gave us $100. Someone gave us $200, and we wound up pulling the money together to do the tour. On Warped, we were playing multiple sets a day, driving, loading in a stage, and sound. It was really hard, hard, hard *work*. With Street Drum Corps, we weren't a touring machine like most bands on regular cycles and stuff. We'd go out and do a tour with the Used, and then we'd be back home for a couple months. But as SDC started to grow, I realized I had to leave theStart. The commitments were becoming too much.

It was through SDC, that I met Dhani Harrison—the son of legendary Beatles guitarist George Harrison—and started playing with him. I did two records with his band thenewno2, and we performed some shows and some stuff in the UK, which was a whole new experience for me. We got to go to his dad's studio in his Friar Park mansion and record a movie score. We did the soundtrack for this major motion picture, *Beautiful Creatures*. Dhani and his right-hand man Paul Hicks wrote the score, and I did all the drumming on it.

I'll never forget it: We walked into the studio and there's two drum kits. Dhani goes, "Which kit do you want to play? That one is Ringo's [Starr, Beatles drummer] and the other one is Jim Keltner's from the Travelling Wilburys." I was like, "I'm playing on both." I was playing those classic kits, in addition to triggering and playing pads to a lot of that stuff: That's the first time I had worked with Ableton on a project. We wound up doing some other gigs. We played this famous venue in Camden Town called Dingwall's and a couple other performances, private things and whatnot.

I got to play Lollapalooza with thenewno2 in 2010, which was absolutely incredible. I got a call from Dhani: He goes, "Hey, Perry Farrell is going to do a pop-up set during Lollapalooza on the Kidzapalooza stage. He wants me to be part of his band. Do you want to come with me?" He says Peter DiStefano from Porno for Pyros is gonna be on guitar, I'm gonna be on drums… and Perry's gonna come up. We did a couple cover songs: a Lou Reed cover, I think an Iggy cover, and Porno for Pyros' "Pets," which is one of my all-time favorite songs. We got offstage and Perry comes up to me and says, "You're amazing: You remind me of Stephen Perkins." Stephen Perkins is one of my favorite drummers and favorite people, *ever.* After that, Jane's Addiction took thenewno2 on tour, and it was incredible to get to share the stage with those guys every night. And Perkins and I became really really good friends. thenewno2 did a tour with Black Rebel Motorcycle Club, we toured with Wolfmother, all good times.

Dhani and I became such great friends. When my wife Lauren and I were planning our wedding, we talked about who we should get to marry us. Dhani was the first person I thought of. We asked him, he accepted, and he killed it. He was incredible. Dhani made it such a magical experience for us and so comforting, you know? He just really owned it. His mom helped him write a portion of his speech, and it was a complete honor to have Olivia Harrison involved. He is somebody I'm still very close with and a great musician to work with.

In the middle of all this excitement, I made my first foray into pop music. Our vision for the Street Drum Corps record was much different than what Interscope wanted. When we told the label, "Hey, we want to go to a remote island or some secluded place and work with Diplo and make a beat-heavy record," the executives were like, "It's too risky. You need to go in with Howard Benson, and you're guaranteed a hit record." We met with Howard, who we respect personally, and we love his work. Coincidentally, we did pre-production with him at Tommy Lee's killer studio in his house in Calabasas. He was on tour, so we rented out his home studio for like a week or two.

Later on, we went into EastWest Studios and spent a week there doing drums and percussion. We're in there recording, and all of a sudden, I notice an attractive blonde girl with Howard in a control room. I come in to listen to the take and he's like, "Frank, this is Orianthi. She was Michael Jackson's guitar player. She just watched you drum and I want you to play on our song. Mark my words, this song is gonna be a number one," blah blah blah. We finished recording Street Drum Corps and I laid down some drum tracks for her single. Months later, I'm at the gym on the treadmill, and the music video for "According to You" comes on—and there are my drums! The song goes to number one and I get my first Gold Record. And then it went Platinum. *Insane*. After that, I became Howard's go-to session drummer and recorded a ton of records with him, including Kelly Clarkson's Platinum-selling *Stronger*.

We finished the SDC record, and then Jared Leto called to put us on the Thirty Seconds to Mars 2010 world tour, featured in the documentary series *Into the Wild*. We are the main support for America, Europe, and the UK. But before we decided to pack our bags for :30TM, we had committed to appearing at Projekt Revolution at the behest of our friends Chester Bennington and Linkin Park. Chester and I had been talking for years about how Linkin Park and Street Drum Corps could work together. He goes, "I've got it. We're doing our Projekt Revolution Tour. I want you guys to open the main stage, so it's something refreshing and different that people see when they come to this festival. And then you guys are Linkin Park's intro, middle, and outro of the show." And we created all these pieces with them to make intros and extended outros and things for their show. Again, we're on tour without any Interscope songs or anything, playing all these unreleased songs.

After I did Projekt Revolution with Street Drum Corps and Linkin Park, Chester had me over for dinner at Ryan Shuck's house with Amir Derakh, who are both in Julien-K. We hit it off really really well. Ryan and I became really close really quickly, and then they asked me to tour with them behind the *We're Here with You* record. They actually made me audition, which was funny. It was weird because I'd show up to auditions, and there's a ton of my Street Drum Corps drummers in the parking lot. And they all saw me and were like, "*Fuck...*" I landed the gig and then went through that whole tour cycle with them in Europe and America.

The whole time I was out with Julien-K, I kept telling them, "You've got to get Dead by Sunrise back together. It's such a great fucking band." The band was essentially Julien-K with Chester on vocals, and they only made one album, *Out of Ashes,* in 2009. Every time I would bring it up, Ryan and Amir's response was... semi-optimistic: "We feel like you could be the person that helps us. Since you're close with Chester and tight with us, you can be the guy championing for this to happen."

We actually had a Julien-K and Street Drum Corps show booked in Arizona together. Chester was living there at the time, and I was like, "Dude! Jump up with Julien-K. We'll do the single ["Crawl Back In"]." Chester was like, "Fuck, yeah." That's what started it. Unfortunately, the show wound up not happening: The promoters pulled the show because it was way too big of a venue and ticket sales did not go so well. But that was going to be the first time Dead by Sunrise played live. Julien-K were rehearsing, getting it ready, and then the show got pulled. Then Chester was back in Linkin Park mode. But we kept talking about it.

Fast forward to when I was in Russia with Sum 41. I walked into some random pub in Red Square to have lunch—and they're playing fucking Dead by Sunrise. I group-texted Amir, Ryan, and Chester. "Guys, we've been talking about this. I'm in a bar in Russia, and they are playing Dead by Sunrise. This is a sign. Let's fucking do this." And everybody was like, "We're down." So we started trying to figure out when schedules and things were going to work for everybody. We unfortunately never got the chance. But it was cool that I got the excitement going again and everybody was starting to have conversations about it.

When I was in Julien-K, those guys would do interviews; they were like "Frank's our drummer. He's in Dead by Sunrise if we do anything again, he's in the band." They were very generous. They put out that one record with Howard Benson that I wasn't on. I saw them perform at K-Rock's Acoustic Christmas and shit like that. But their drummer had retired and became a tattoo artist, had kids, and was not doing music anymore.

When Chester passed away, I was literally onstage soundchecking with Sum 41 in Canada, right after the night I won at the AP Awards. I woke up the next day after winning the award and I sent Chester the footage of me, Adrian, and Josh performing our set. He had just taken his kids to see twenty one pilots; they were huge fans. I sent him the email, went to the airport, flew to Canada, and got onstage at soundcheck. My manager called me and told me about his passing before it went public. I remember being told by the tour manager, "Frank, we've got soundcheck. Get off the phone." I just found out Chester passed. He had already passed when I sent him that email. So I don't even think he got to see it.

I learned so much on Projekt Revolution. How cool Chester was, how professional the entire Linkin Park camp was, and just being able to have been part of that. After Chester passed, the Linkin Park guys announced there would be a memorial show at the Hollywood Bowl. I sent Mike Shinoda messages saying that I'd love to be involved in any way possible. He's like, "Absolutely!" I showed up and was so prepared and eager to help. "We want to do a whole added percussion thing on two songs. Come to rehearsal. Bring your drum kit but bring a bunch of extra toms and stuff." I got on the phone with their drummer Rob Bourdon, and we came up with parts to put drum moments into two of their songs.

I'm at rehearsal and Mike Shinoda asks, "Hey, do you also want to play on the song that we have with Steve Aoki ["A Light That Never Comes"]?" I'm like, "Yeah, man!" It had more of an EDM Linkin Park vibe. Then Mike says, "We're doing the song that System of a Down wrote with us from *The Hunting Party* record. Do you want to play on that song?" *Hell, yeah!* So there I was, rehearsing with Shavo and Daron from System of a Down, playing "Rebellion" with Linkin Park. Rob was like, "Can you play the song with System? Because I just don't have bandwidth right now. I'm mourning. I'm overwhelmed." Dude, I got your back.

And then I wound up having Deryck Whibley be part of one of the songs at the last minute. They needed a vocalist for "The Catalyst," and I was telling Deryck about it. He's like, "I can do it, man. I've got the same range." He came in and crushed it. So we got to do that together, which was super-super-special to honor Chester's legacy and everything that night.

I showed up and I was down to do whatever they needed. I let all these other talented artists (Travis Barker, Zedd, Adrian) use my gear to help the production team out. I ended up playing four songs. And I got to play the Hollywood Bowl: Forget about it being a "first," that was a bucket list item. It was just a team-player thing, but it was like, holy shit! I'm walking around: all these rock stars are playing with *my* kit. I'm fist-bumping Travis Barker, because Blink's playing the show, too. And you know, we're honoring our friend here…

Sometimes I still just see myself as the little kid from Long Island who always wanted to do this. I feel like I'm still on that path I set for myself. But it's incredible when you take a step back and just think about it all. And it all happened in California. Whether it's the Long Island covers scene or judgmental managers in gear stores, I'm not going back.

CHRISTIE POIRIER: Frank is always on the go. He's got that New York mentality, you know? Which is good. It gets things done. I think that's why he made it so quickly in California: He wasn't waiting for anybody.

3
STREET DRUM CORPS

I attached the tiniest U-Haul trailer possible to my Nissan Sentra and played my last gig with The Zoo at the Dublin Pub in New Hyde Park, Long Island. I got offstage at 3:30 in the morning, threw my drum kit in the trailer, and drove my ass to Los Angeles. I had a show, so I had to be there really quickly.

I brought Scott Zant, the bass player from The Zoo, with me. He quit the cover band and moved with me because it didn't work out with our LA bass player. I vouched for Scott and got him the gig. He tossed his bass in the back of the trailer, and off we went at 4:00 in the morning, racing toward LA, ready to take shifts driving and sleeping.

So we hit Texas. As you know, Texas takes about a day to drive through. And we're in El Paso… sorry, not El Paso, Odessa. It's my turn to drive. I wake up, Scott's shift is done, and I go fill up the car with gas and drive away. Just as I'm about to get on the freeway, the car makes some crazy sound I've never heard before. I see smoke. *I'm like, that's not good.* I pulled off to the side of the road and called my best friend, Mike Gabriel, who I grew up with. His dad owned a mechanic shop, and Mike worked there. I tell him what's happening, and he's like, "You blew the head gasket." OK, that's bad.

I'm looking around and I see there's a gas station with a U-Haul dealer. I pull in, unload the trailer into a U-Haul box truck, and grab one of those car trailers to haul my car. This all happened in minutes, and we were back on the road.

We literally drove straight to the first show. We didn't even have time to get to my shitty, roach-infested apartment in Koreatown or do anything else. We drove to the first show and you can imagine… in Hollywood… pulling up in a big U-Haul truck with a car hooked up to the back, trying to unload and load into a small bar to play a show.

And that's how my journey began in LA. Oh, and we actually found out later that the gas station in Odessa had their gas pumps backwards. So unfortunately I had put diesel fuel in my car, and it had blown the head gasket. All the hard-earned money that I had saved—because as we know, you need a reliable car in LA to get around to gigs and go to meetings—went into fixing that damn car, and I was fucking broke. This band better happen, and it better happen quick.

I immediately shifted into showcase mode that night and thought, "It's OK. It's gonna be great." The singer-songwriter we were working with had what they used to call a development deal. A production company had funded a polished, finished record. (They got the guy who I think did The Killers' first big record to mix.) It was all ready to go; she just needed to put together a band to show that she could perform live. And I was thinking, "OK, well I don't have any money, but we're about to do these showcases, and then we're gonna be off to the races—a success story."

I had watched so many of the cover band guys snag record deals or land big gigs in an LA band. And when it didn't work out, they would get discouraged and come back home with their tails between their legs, returning to the cover band scene as the jaded musicians we all know too well. So I was like, *I am not going to become one of these Long Island guys. I'm going to make it. I'm gonna go there and give this everything I have.* This band literally has a finished record, has an artist deal. We just need to put the band together, showcase, boom!

But quickly after we showcased, we realized it was not going well. She choked. And that's when the panic set in because there was no Plan B. I went out there banking on this to succeed, and when it didn't, I realized I needed to hustle for some money. I tried to get a job at Guitar Center. I couldn't land any job, *anywhere*.

I had met Bobby and Adam Alt at one of the club gigs she played. They were friends with the guitar player in that band. We ended our set with Jane's Addiction's "Three Days," and they jumped up on my floor toms for a wild tribal drum thing to end the show. I just kept seeing those guys in the same circles. Adam's band, Circus Minor, would open for us at showcases, and we kept bumping into each other at parties. That's when they invited me to check out their percussion show, Bobby & Adam Alt's Experiment. They had a drum circle event at Remo Percussion Center, and they kicked off their show by playing on pots and pans. And that's when the light bulb went on.

Right after that event, we drove that night to San Luis Obispo to see my buddy John Sawicki play in *Stomp*. Our minds were blown, and we were feeling inspired. After the show, we all went to a bar with the cast of *Stomp*. The DJs killed the music, and they went into the kitchen and brought out all the bar kegs and pots and pans, whatever they could find. We just dove in, no plans at all. It was like "one, two, three, four…" and we launched into this crazy drum jam. We took over the whole fucking place. Dancing girls were grinding on us! It was magical. On the whole drive home from St. Louis Obispo, Bobby and Adam were like, "OK, we've got something here. We gotta do something about this."

That's when we hatched a plan. The next day, we met at the junkyard across from Bobby's rehearsal studio. Adam knows how to film and edit, so we figured let's shoot a whole day of us in the junkyard running around, going nuts slamming car doors, playing on dumpsters—whatever. Adam would edit it down, and we'd send it around. I knew the theme park world because that's what I was doing in Hershey Park before I moved to California.

When I was working in Pennsylvania, I started my own solo drum show. I did a couple of theme parks, but it never really took off. The problem was, where I lived, it was cold, so you only have summer seasons there. Here, though, the theme parks have entertainment year-round because it's warm. Now, I'm gonna date myself here: I sent VHS tapes of SDC to Universal Studios and Six Flags Magic Mountain. Universal hired us to do CityWalk, creating a street-performer atmosphere where we would just make tips. After we did that, Six Flags offered us a residency every single weekend for the whole summer. And then *that* went so well that they offered us a residency for their Halloween event. Then Bobby sent a tape to Kevin Lyman and his music staff (because Bobby played drums in S.T.U.N., he knew all those people), and then Kevin invited us on the Warped Tour. So really, we didn't think shit was gonna happen, and all of a sudden, *everything happened*.

So that was my job. I was playing drums on the weekend at a theme park with Street Drum Corps. That's where we were building our routines, and because we didn't have a formal show, we were just street performers. But we started coming up with routines and choreography: That's where we built the show and then put together a mini-set that we could tour with on Warped and all that kind of stuff. But it wasn't full-on yet; it was still just summer-only on weekends.

That's when Bobby said, "Hey, theStart just lost their drummer. You should go audition." I went and auditioned, got that gig, and I was piggybacking between Start gigs and Street Drum Corps until SDC became big enough that I had to step down from theStart. I was doing something that was for fun, something I never thought I would make a dollar doing, you know? But there was just something there. We were inspired and we just went with it. It happened quickly: I didn't have to get a real job because Street Drum Corps became my job.

It wasn't long before SDC became so in demand that we had to create franchises. Everyone called them "franchises," but I honestly think that wasn't the right word. We would get hired by, let's say, five theme parks, and we would bring in five sets of local drummers. We would train them, put them on a payroll, and they'd do our show. So it's not a franchise like McDonald's, where someone pays X amount and here's the manual and training to run it. That's a different thing. We would call it that, but technically I don't think that's the real term. "Subcontractor," maybe?

We were still very hands-on. During the Halloween season, I'd fly around from theme park to theme park training these drummers—and that was the coolest part. Seeing these kids in the middle of fucking Shakopee, Minnesota, who had never even hit a keg in their life. But after a week and a half of me friggin' training them, these kids were fuckin' beatin' the shit out of that junk and bein' rock stars. That was what it was about for me. To see these kids, and then all of a sudden they're at the show, and there's a line of people waiting for their autographs. They're now rock stars in their town at the theme park. For me, that was really fuckin' cool.

Think about it: So many other companies in that world are like, "OK, we're gonna do your theme park. But we're going to hire drummers. We're going to ship them out, you're going to put them up and house them." And I was like, *fuck that.* There are enough talented drummers in every fucking town and city. Let's save the theme park money on lodging and flights and have these kids commute locally. You're within an hour's drive because most theme parks are in the middle of fucking nowhere. Let's give local drummers the job. That made it harder for us because yeah, in LA, I could have hired 50 drummers, trained them, and then just sent them out to all the theme parks. They could have lived there, but fuck that. I made it hard on myself and hired local everywhere, while all these other fucking companies just hire people from New York and LA, ship them out, and let them live there. They're costing these theme parks so much money. And I was like, *that's bullshit.* That's copping out. We're gonna dig deep and get local talent. These kids might not be the greatest drummers in the world, but after a week with me training them, they're gonna be. And it was fucking awesome.

That's something I was so proud of doing with Street Drum Corps that all these other companies wouldn't. We were at Six Flags Great Adventure in New Jersey for five years doing our Halloween show. I'm not involved anymore, but there's a show now called Blade Drums. They basically hired a company to rip off our show. They're playing grinders, they're beating kegs, they've got a fire performer. OK, Street Drum Corps, we didn't create any of that shit. We couldn't copyright it. But other people are doing what we did in that world now. I'll take it as flattery.

But that's not what it was solely about. We were giving drummers jobs being drummers instead of bagging groceries. We were all these places at once, and we never said no to a gig. You needed five Street Drum Corps on the same day in five different states? You got it.

Anyway, we would sit in Bobby's bedroom on the floor with our computers and figure out, "How are we going to go on the Warped Tour? What companies are we going to hit up?" So we're cold-calling, emailing, "Hey, we're this new group! We're going to Warped Tour, and we're going to promote your brand to help us do this tour," all that stuff. This was back when we couldn't afford a tour manager: We had to figure out van rentals, trailer rentals, and how the hell hotels worked. We had to print out 100 pages of fucking MapQuest directions to get from show to show!

Kevin Lyman was like, "I love you guys. You can come on Warped Tour, but I don't have a stage for you. You have to figure it out on your own." So we brought our own stage. We had to build it. We had to bring our own sound. We were driving in a van and trailer and not sleeping—like the whole deal. Kevin was the one that said, "Hey, we play all these fairgrounds. You guys should have all your drum groups at the fairs." He's the one that sparked that idea.

We had our mascot—Bert McCracken of The Used—to help launch our career. Bless that man's soul! We fucking went for it. We played three sets a day. While the other bands played one set a day, we were hanging out with *everybody.* It was 2005, the year that Warped Tour had what I'd consider its biggest, most mainstream lineup they've ever had. It was My Chemical Romance, Fall Out Boy, The Offspring, Transplants—like a fucking massive lineup that year. I mean, we worked so hard on that tour and it went over so well.

Kevin gave us a record deal on Warcon. That was the first record deal I ever had in my life. Kevin and Warcon co-founder Bob Chiappardi asked us to pick a song for the label's holiday-themed comp, *The Taste of Christmas*, and McCracken chose John Lennon and Yoko Ono's "Happy Xmas (War Is Over)." We were invited by Yoko to perform it at the 2005 New York Chapter of the Recording Academy Honors show. Seeing her offstage singing, dancing, and crying was a special high point for us.

And then Kevin put us on his Taste of Chaos tour, where we played packed arenas as we supported Deftones every night. And then years later, I joined Sum 41, and my first American tour with them was the entire Warped Tour.

Kevin said one of the most meaningful things anyone has ever said to me in my entire life. He told me, "What you put into it is what you get out of it. If you come on the Warped Tour and you're just gonna hide in your fucking van or bus or car all day and just go out and do your set, good luck. Hopefully, your live show will connect with people, and that's enough to get you to the finish line. But if you're out there meeting kids at the booth, hanging out and meeting bands, working the line and all that kind of stuff, you're really going to get so much more out of it." That really resonated with me.

KEVIN LYMAN, founder of Vans Warped Tour:
You can tell that Frank wasn't ever going to just "settle." Not settle, but maybe *just* be in a band. He was always going to want to try new things, use his craft and the work he's been doing with SJC Drums as a mentor and teacher, you know? He's always been someone who is always in constant motion, if that makes sense. Some people would have been complacent being a drummer in Sum 41. Where so many would just say, "I'm in this band, this is what I do," that's great, but he was always trying to do other things too, through his educational programs he's done with SJC. I've always been quite impressed with what he's accomplished.

Warcon put out the Street Drum Corps record. I was talking to them about how they could potentially franchise that at one point. Like having multiple groups across the country and becoming the Blue Man Group of street drumming. I had a palette of those albums, and when Warcon was folding up, I just called them one day and told them to come grab those records, *just take them*, you know? They said they probably made more money than they ever would have on a record deal by just giving them those CDs and then they would sell them at Six Flags Magic Mountain.

There's a certain kind of mentality that goes with LA, and there's a certain type of mentality that goes with New York. The way I always describe it is when you go to LA, you have meetings to schedule more meetings. When you go to New York, you're always on the hustle, and no one's wasting your time. And you only get a chance to waste people's time *once*. Frank doesn't wait to do anything. He has an idea or somebody brings something up, and he's immediately like, "Well, how do we make that happen? What do we say? Where do we go? What do we do, what do we need?" He's immediately running it. He's running it through his head, but still thinking about it at the same time. I was trying to think of a great story about someone who creates a lot of drama, but Frank's not that person. Frank takes what he does seriously, but he also realizes that you don't have to be overly serious. We're producing music. We're entertaining people. I don't remember ever having any drama with Frank, which is, of itself, a great story.

I would talk to people in bands I was friendly with. SDC got on those Linkin Park and Thirty Seconds to Mars tours because they liked the ideas I pitched. I told them that SDC would be your changeover act to hype up the crowd, so it wouldn't just be like house lights on with an iPod playing. Then we'd enhance their show and be part of the performance as these crazy drummers doing extra stuff. That's how we got on all those tours and built our reputation: Thirty Seconds to Mars took us around the world. Linkin Park took us on Projekt Revolution. We were just shooting for the moon, going to these huge artists and offering them something—and they were all into it. We got to create these epic drum moments in their shows and tours and do stuff that most young bands—especially some dudes playing buckets—would never have been given the opportunity to do.

Bands would fight over us. Jared Leto saw us on The Used tour, then he took us on his tour. Then we were out with Matisyahu, and they were like, "You're coming on our tour after that. We need you." And it was this fun thing that started happening. But then it got to a point where, once we got big enough, when we signed with Interscope, we stopped being the changeover act. We started opening the show with a proper set. We were actually main support for 30STM playing fucking Wembley arena. We're the main support, and then we would be part of their show. We went from this little 15-minute hype thing to actually opening the show with a proper set or being named support and then playing with the headliner to enhance their shows.

We pitched Interscope on the Las Vegas show. Jimmy Iovine was all in. You know, Street Drum Corps got the first 360 deal at Interscope. It took fucking forever to make the deal because it didn't exist yet. Iovine bought into SDC. He was an owner/partner. What happened was his Beats headphone thing blew up, and then he was on his way out of A&R. We went through four different A&R guys and only released one single on Interscope. We were touring the world as main support to Thirty Seconds to Mars and didn't have a record out, didn't have tour support. Such a missed opportunity, because we were playing sold-out fucking arenas and going over huge.

When we got back from that tour, everything fell apart. Our manager, John Reese, quit on us. Interscope didn't renew our deal after telling us not to do the franchises and theme park gigs, insisting, "You need to just focus on being this hit band with hit songs. It all starts with a hit song…"

So I just said, "I'm gonna manage the fucking band."

And that's exactly what I did. Without the help of a major label or a high profile manager, SDC flourished. Not only did we have a record number of touring franchises crisscrossing the country, we secured a Las Vegas residency at the Hard Rock Hotel & Casino in 2013, and we teamed up with AEG to fulfill a personal dream of building a sinister haunted house in "Scared in New Jersey" in 2017. And all it took was nearly all my free time in dim hotel rooms and travelling in compact tour bunks between gigs.

And a fuck-ton of roaming charges. And a good part of my mind.

4
WALKING WITH GIANTS

Street Drum Corps is still in a developmental stage, and attempts at securing a day job seem even more futile. Fortunately, I fall into the orbits of some legendary players seeking drummers. And while it feels like I've been living out of a suitcase for months or even years, the experiences will definitely stay with me indefinitely.

As all this is happening, Bobby Alt tells me he is good friends with the band theStart, and they needed a drummer. Bobby's like, "You gotta go audition." I go and audition, and I immediately get the gig. They were going on a full-blown, headlining US tour. I said I'll take the gig, but I can't do the first weekend of the tour because that's the last weekend of this theme park residency. They said, no worries, "We have someone who can sub."

So we were about to start rehearsals for theStart tour. Since they were signed to Nitro—the label founded by Dexter Holland from The Offspring—we were going to rehearse at his facility. I walk in and the drummer who's going to sub for me is there. The band is rehearsing with both of us. I walk over and look at the drum set next to mine. It says NO DOUBT on the kick drum. The band explains to me that Adrian Young of No Doubt is "gonna do the first weekend for you. He's a big fan of our band and he's a friend." Talk about being intimidated. I'm in The Offspring's personal rehearsal studio, and Adrian from No Doubt is here. *Whoa.*

I meet Adrian, and we hit it off immediately. He does the first weekend, and I go finish the weekend of SDC shows. It just so happened that the tour kickoff for theStart tour was at Chain Reaction in Anaheim. Adrian does the show while I play at Magic Mountain with SDC's Halloween drum show.

I make it in time to see their encore at Chain Reaction, driving from Valencia to Anaheim. The show's sold out, and the crowd's chanting for an encore. Adrian doesn't know any more songs: He learned the set, but the crowd wants another one, so they literally call me out on the microphone. I fight my way through the crowd, jump up onstage, and play two songs with them. My first show with theStart, with Adrian standing there, side-stage.

I come offstage into the dressing room. Adrian looks at me and goes, "Dude,

I just played the whole show. You came up and played two songs, and you just totally kicked my ass. Like, I gotta go home now and really practice because I'm gonna sub for you next weekend." It was just mind-blowing—Adrian, who I idolized, is giving me props like this.

ADRIAN YOUNG, No Doubt/DREAMCAR drummer/producer:
Frank works his ass off. If he's having a bad day, I don't know it. I've never seen it. He keeps his chin up, right? And not everybody has that capability.

I first met Frank because I got asked to sub a couple gigs for this band called theStart. I knew they had gotten a new drummer named Frank. I didn't know Frank at the time, and then he came by the rehearsal space and we met. At that gig I played with the band, he was there. We came out to do an encore, and I already played all the songs I knew. I didn't know any more of their set, so Frank hopped up on the drum set. I saw him play and I thought, "Oh, so this young man from New York is a beast." Frank's always been a pretty high-energy dude, mainly from just the work ethic point of view and, like I said, he's always got his chin up looking for positives in any situation. So he didn't come off like an East Coast tough guy to me so much. Besides, there's plenty of testosterone out in California, so the generalizations are kind of humorous, I think.

Well, in the beginning we'd mainly just talk about drums, just hanging out and having beers—you know, being dudes. Very caveman. I think I'm about 10 years older than him, so I had kids before he did. And then later on when he had kids, I got to spend a little time with his growing family when we attended the APMAS award show together in Cleveland. So the bonding changed. We weren't as young and we were less knuckleheaded, so to speak. He's just such a proud, happy dad. And I could clearly see that his partying days were behind him. Not that he ever had a major issue with it, but he was just laser-focused and happy.

He's a pretty selfless guy. When Street Drum Corps was doing their record, Frank was the main point person of the project. Maybe the only drum set person in the band at that moment. He says to me, "Hey, would you be into playing drums on a song," meaning he's going to step aside. Which is pretty selfless because there are a lot of drummers who are too ego-driven to even consider something like that, you know? They'd be like, "Nope, I'm the drummer, no one else is playing, I'll do all the songs." I think that openness showed a lot. I don't know if I could be that open saying I'm going to have someone else play drums on a No Doubt song. And it struck me that he would even make that suggestion.

I remember putting together the "Drum Moment" for the AP Awards. Frank calls me and says, "I have this idea. What if you and I do this drum thing, but we also have [twenty one pilots drummer] Josh Dun join us. We'll do a three-person drum performance." And I was like, "Yeah, let's do that. That sounds awesome." And because of Frank's experience with SDC, he's good at organizing drum movements and performances with multiple players. So he took the lead on that. And it was super-fun. I loved it. I really enjoyed the process because Frank and Josh would come to my house and we just started making up parts and rehearsing. The process was enjoyable because I like those guys: they're really good dudes and, of course, the performance part of it is really awesome.

Frank must've been on cloud nine that night. He had his family out there, he did his performance, and he won the Best Drummer award, all on the same night. I remember, when they were announcing the nominees for that award—I think there were six—I was just like "get it, get it, get it, Frank." And then when they announced it, I was like, "Yes! Yes!"

I first met Chester Bennington backstage at the MySpace.com 2nd Anniversary concert. He was talking to the guys in Jimmy Eat World, who we were sharing a dressing room with. He had seen SDC a few times and loved us. We were chatting a few years later, and he told me, "We're doing our Projekt Revolution tour and I want you guys to open the mainstage because I don't want there to be a band when people come in, I want it to be something different. Linkin Park wants you guys to be part of the show, where you're our intro, our middle, our outro." So, Chester and I dreamt up that whole thing, his band signed off on it, and out we went.

On that tour, Chris Cornell was the main support to Linkin Park. Every day, right as we were playing, he would always be side-stage watching us. He came over to us to introduce himself, and he's like, "I think you guys are gonna be the next big thing. I love what's going on here. You guys want to come onstage and play 'Spoonman' with me every night?" *Fuck, yeah!* So we played our own set, we played "Spoonman" with him, then we were part of Linkin Park's show; this was one of the best tours I've ever done in my life.

Adrian loved Street Drum Corps, and whenever we had a show with special guests, he would show up and perform with us. We were doing this big concert together with Adrian and Street Drum Corps for a Guitar Center/Drum Off concert, and he was like, "Hey man, I was with Tommy Lee the other day and was telling him about you guys. He looked some stuff up and thought it was rad. I need to link you with him—and we should invite him to come watch the performance."

In the late '90s, John Sawicki, one of my best friends from childhood, met Tommy on tour with *Stomp*. Mötley and the *Stomp* cast were staying at the same hotel. And I think when the two of them were partying one night, he got on his phone and went, "Hey Tommy, this is my buddy, Frank." We exchanged pleasantries on speakerphone, and later, we exchanged some emails—then nothing for years. Then, through SDC (and Adrian), Tommy and I connected again and quickly became good friends. We just hit it off so well. SDC were on the Linkin Park tour, and Mötley played the next day at Blossom Music Center outside of Cleveland, Ohio, the same venue as us. We had the day off, so we stayed. That next day was the first time I met him in person and experienced his wild backstage party stuff, and we just hit it off. It was amazing to finally meet my idol and connect on a friendship level. He was the sweetest, raddest rockstar ever.

When our manager John Reese left management to go back to being a festival promoter, we wound up hiring Tommy's manager, Carl Stubner. I was on tour with Dhani Harrison and got a call from Carl. He goes "Scott Weiland's drummer has to miss a bunch of shows, and I want you to fill in." Carl wound up getting me the gig with Scott. The tour was called "Purple to the Core," celebrating the anniversary of those two Stone Temple Pilots records, and I wound up doing a bunch of festivals and one-offs with Scott.

So before I did the Scott Weiland gig, and right before Dhani, Street Drum Corps was recording our Interscope record with Howard Benson. I had finished my drum tracks, so I was gonna go take a break and visit the Mötley tour. Tommy's oldest son was gonna travel with me, and we were just gonna go visit and hang. It was all set to go.

I woke up the next morning and my phone was just loaded with all these missed calls, missed texts, missed emails. They were from Tommy, his tech, and his assistant, saying, "Hey, I had an accident with fireworks last night. You need to come now and fill in for me." I thought it was a joke. I was like, *this can't be real. What is going on?* Sure enough, Tommy's on the phone, saying, "Go grab my son on your way to the airport and get out here."

This is the *Dr. Feelgood* anniversary tour. They're playing the whole record, and I hadn't heard those deep album cuts in a long time. (I got that CD from my dad as a reward for mowing the lawn, trimming the trees, all that yard work.) I played that record endlessly, but I didn't remember a lot of the deep tracks. So I'm blasting the music in my house while I'm packing frantically to go to the airport. Then I had the flight to go over the set. We take a red-eye and land in Boston around six or seven in the morning, and it's almost an hour's drive to the venue from there.

So I show up and I go check out Tommy's drum kit and make sure everything's comfortable. I sit down behind his kit, thinking that because he's so tall, everything was gonna be out of a comfortable reach. I'm super-short compared to him, but he actually plays everything really low and sits low, so I didn't have to move a thing.

Because at this point I've only met Nikki Sixx once or twice *maybe*, I ask Tommy if he can take me around to everyone's dressing rooms and buses, so I can meet everybody. He took me around and everyone was so calm and cool. They don't give me advice, they simply tell me to "just have fun." I'm thinking, *Wow, these guys have a lot of trust. They don't even know me.* Tommy's vouching for me, obviously.

Tommy gave me a couple pointers on stuff like intros and outros. He has electronics and triggers, as well. ("Hey, which pad starts the motorcycle sample on 'Girls, Girls Girls'?") So he and I go through everything. He was hidden side-stage for the show and had a microphone so he could talk to me through my in-ears to tell me, for example, if there was an extended outro for another six bars before the ending, stuff like that. He was the air traffic controller who got me through the stuff that was a little bit different live. Which was incredibly helpful.

Then towards the middle of the show, he's like, "You got this," and just started having fun since he couldn't play. He was just partying, and then I'd do something cool or whatever and he'd be yelling something in my in-ears because he's stoked about my playing. I'm like, "Dude! I'm tryin' to play your gig, stop screaming in my ears! Ha!" Later, he got to go to the soundboard and listen to the band out there for the first time ever. He put his hoodie up so nobody would notice him, and he got to hear his own band playing live. It was a trip for him because we play similarly; I grew up learning by watching him and all the stuff he did. So it just *felt* like he was up there with the band, you know?

After we played the *Dr. Feelgood* album, there was a moment when the crew changed the whole stage set around, and then we came back out and performed all the other big singles from the other records. So, for that moment, Tommy had a quick-change room with his tech in it, and I was in there with them. Suddenly, all the band guys come in and Tommy's like, "What the hell? They've never come in here before." And they all were like, "Thank you. We feel like we're playing with Tommy, so we're not worried about the gig. It's a pleasure to play with you. You're crushing it. Thank you!" And I was just like, *holy shit.*

I think the coolest part was the huddle. The whole stage was blacked out and it was designed to look like we were playing in a padded cell in an insane asylum room, because it was *Dr. Feelgood.* So it was super-tight quarters, and we all went in there and I'm bumping fists with Vince Neil, Mick Mars, and Nikki Sixx. I counted in "Dr. Feelgood" and we were off! I was literally smiling and screaming. Every emotion was pouring out.

At one point, Nikki came over the drum riser, giving me the full "bring it" attitude. I was sitting there yelling back at him and it was such a special moment to connect with one of my idols onstage. At this moment in time, there is absolutely no difference between 5-year-old Frank and 31-year-old Frank.

After the show, I grabbed my phone and called my mom. I put her on speaker and Tommy's like, "He fucking crushed it," and he's telling my mom how I did. I remember him showing me a text message that Nikki sent saying thanks for bringing me onboard. Then a couple of days later, I'm in the dressing room getting body work done because it's a two-hour set and I was going so hard. They had a girl working on my arms, and in the background, I'm hearing Mick Mars do an interview. The journalist is asking him how it's going without Tommy, and Mick just said the most amazing things about me. "It just feels like Tommy's up there. He's crushing it, he's a pro." And I'm like, *is this real life*?

My Zummo family (father, godfather, and aunt) was at the show in Tampa, Florida. Tommy told the crowd about me filling in for him due to his injury, as well as the story of how my father took me to see Mötley, at age 5, for my first concert ever—and now my dad is in the crowd watching his son play with Mötley. The crowd erupted. My dad was standing on his seat high-fiving everyone and they were handing him free beers. After my father passed, Mötley's production manager, Robert Long, sent me the video of Tommy and that moment from the show. The memory is now on my YouTube to be saved forever.

TOMMY LEE, drummer for Mötley Crüe and solo artist:

The older I get, the more I actually realize and feel and sort of digest that sense of legacy and inspiration. To have inspired somebody that much, to go and have them achieve something for themselves is just overwhelming. That's how Frank makes me feel. He just makes me eternally happy. It's wonderful. It's beautiful. It's weird!

Frank is a fucking hustler! He goes after shit and you gotta love him for that. I'm incredibly humbled and I love that I've had such a big impact on him. That's a lot to say, especially these days. There's this special connection... We all have influences. Shit, I've been influenced by some great drummers, and a few of them I've never met. I never met my hero, John Bonham. But Frank and I, we're friends. He filled in for me when I injured myself and we shared a lot of things other than music, and that's a pretty powerful connection. At the end of the day, to have that bond with somebody that you either looked up to or inspired you is incredibly rare. Because I didn't really have that: I didn't get to meet any of my heroes until much later on. That puts things in perspective for myself and for Frank.

Just knowing him and working in the studio with him, I knew what he was capable of. When we needed the guy, I knew that he was the only call. He already knew all of the stuff. There was no audition period or panic like, "Oh boy, I hope we can get all this material together," you know? Because it was an emergency, I was like, "If anybody's gonna pull this, Frank's gonna to pull it." And he was on the first flight over, the next day.

What does Frank excel at? A really cool word is "adapting." He seems to, you know, take whatever might seem difficult or even impossible and just fucking *adapt*. Especially with Sum 41. Frank has been inspired by so much: pop, punk-rock pop, pop-punk. And for some reason, he just really sat into that and made those styles his. He takes the task at hand and makes it his.

I'm just gonna just drop some love off right here. It's a good time to congratulate him on his success and helping Sum 41 do their due diligence there. He's become quite the guy. He's got a family now, and he's very different from when we first met. Thanks, Frank!

When I got the Mötley gig, the press totally blew up for that. Because SDC were on Interscope at that point, the label's publicist put out press releases announcing that I was filling in for Tommy. And you know that that *really* spread in the industry. It did amazing things for my career, because I became known as the guy that can fill in at the last minute and deliver. When I got home from that tour, Dhani Harrison asked me to start touring with thenewno2. So I immediately transitioned into touring with Dhani.

While I'm on the road, I get a call to go play with Scott Weiland.

I was on tour with him and I witnessed firsthand just how far darkness could go. When I got the Weiland gig, I was told by the tour manager, "Hey, just so you know what you're getting into. Let's just say the lights are on, but no one's home." That was the analogy I was given. Definitely Scott was up, he was down. His death wasn't a shock.

I was supposed to be on that tour when he died. I couldn't do it, though, and it's a fucking blessing, because I didn't want to be on that bus or around when that happened. He was a lovely person: He was so sweet to me and we had great times. But you could see the roller coaster. I was so glad that I wasn't there because that would have traumatized me. The guy who replaced me—Joey Castillo, who used to be in Queens of the Stone Age and Danzig—is the one who found Scott dead. We talked about it backstage in London on Halloween when The Bronx opened for Sum on the last UK tour. For hours, we just talked about Scott and just everything that went on.

The universe told me that I needed to be with my new wife, get married, go on my honeymoon, and have family time—not be a part of this toxic situation. I played rad shows with Scott. I had great times with him. But I knew, when I rode a bus with him for one night, this wasn't going to be a healthy tour to be on. And Joey's been sober forever, and he was on this bus. I wasn't sober then, but I wasn't an addict; I would have some drinks to relax. I used to just be by myself in my bunk. The second we got to the venue or hotel, I'd be off and I'd just distance myself.

There's a video on my YouTube where we're playing "Wicked Garden," and Scott—third fuckin' song—he just turns around. This is my first time meeting him onstage. There was no rehearsal. I never met him before the show. We're onstage, and he just turns around, locks eyes with me, and sings the rest of the song to me with his back to the audience. Then he goes on a rant to the audience about how great I am and how he saw my YouTube videos. I found out much later that Scott had seen one of my shows with Mötley and decided I had to be in the band…

He was very to himself, hanging out with his wife, but then he would come hang out with us after the show and stuff. We would just hang out and talk—if he was in the mood. If he had a bad day or a bad show, he'd be gone. I didn't tour with him extensively enough to be in that situation. But I know all the guys that were in the band loved being there because they were also like his party pals, you know? Jeremy Brown was the guitarist when I joined Weiland's band. He died too: he mixed some shit, went to bed, didn't wake up. Accidental. Same thing happened to Scott, a year later or something. The bass player, Tommy Black, and I are the only ones still alive from that band.

At that same time, Chester was in Stone Temple Pilots while I was playing with Scott. We were sharing stories back and forth about all that. We were both geeking out that we were playing with these legends. But I also think that was still at a time when mental health wasn't discussed as openly as it is now.

As all this is happening, during SDC's biggest residency, my dear friend Dave Zonshine (who manages thenewno2 and also helped SDC get the Interscope deal), starts managing Gary Numan. He tells me Gary's drummer has a family emergency, and he needs me to tour with Gary. I'm on the road at this time, training our groups for the Halloween theme park shows, and I'm doing the Vegas residency. I'm flying from one theme park to the next to Vegas. I'm all over the place. And now I'm playing with Gary Numan.

How good is this: My first shows with Gary were two nights at the Hollywood Forever Cemetery. After the second show, I got on a flight out to Las Vegas to perform at the Hard Rock Casino with Street Drum Corps to meet our residency.

I will say that Gary is one of the most fucking punk-rock, non-diva artists I've ever worked with. He'll play fucking seven shows in a row: he won't complain. He's the most lovely, caring, sweet person on tour. His wife was on the tour—she's hysterical! We became really good friends and we had such respect for each other. I invited him to my wedding and he came—it was super-special.

But just playing those songs and getting to be part of it, that was really fucking incredible. It was pretty special. It was just really fucking rad to see an artist at that age and level just being like, *let's fucking go*. It was pretty inspiring.

GARY NUMAN, electronic rock music innovator/producer:
My own drummer had pulled out at the last minute for some health reasons or something else. I was very briefly managed by somebody several years ago, and I think that Frank was working for him through another band—might have been Dhani Harrison. There was a very temporary, short-notice hiccup. The manager said, "I know someone," and that was Frank.

You know, it's quite a scary thing when you've got somebody you *don't* know being recommended by somebody you *barely* know to fit in on very short notice. Within the first 10 minutes, I was massively relieved. Frank knew every song. His professionalism was just shocking, just amazing. I don't remember if it was a day or two—it might have been a week, I can't remember—but it was not much time to learn a complete set of something that he didn't know. And that was impressive.

The way he played them was different to the genre that I'd been using for a very, very long time, and yet they fit perfectly. I was grateful for his enthusiasm. Sometimes you work with a lot of people and they're very, very good. They know they're very good and they come in and they're sort of jaded. They've done it all before, seen it all before, and they don't care. It's just a job. And they bring that attitude with them.

But if you've got someone who comes in and they're bright, and they're breezy and they're enthusiastic and suggest things, and are complimentary, and are clearly happy to be there, that's a lovely thing. It's a nice person to work with and it gives you a fantastic foundation to work on any little changes that you might want to make. Frank was an absolute golden find. I love Frankie. I'm forever grateful for the way he came in, the way he approached it, the enthusiasm, the professionalism, just an incredibly likable person to be around.

He was great fun to tour with. He is always upbeat, always happy, always contributing. I would find it very difficult to understand how anyone could not get on with Frank. In any situation, he's a very pleasant person to be around. No obvious ego whatsoever. He was fantastic to his crew, the people that were helping him set up the drums. Obviously his setup was very different to what they knew before so they had to learn what he wanted with drum positioning and so on. But again, there was nothing aggressive or egotistic about him whatsoever. He is just a genuinely nice person that loves what he does.

And he was always fun to be with. Always interesting, had no end of anecdotes, always kind. The thing that I really noticed about Frank, none of his stories were negative. *None.* He must have had them but he doesn't relay them, he only relays positive things, good things that happen to him. He's got nothing but good things to say about the people he knows and cares for. He's a lovely person who happens to be a really brilliant drummer. He's got it all going for him, and he's one of the people I've been most pleased to have known in the years I've done this. I've met an awful lot of people, since I've been doing this now for 47 years, and I've seen more than my share of shitbags. Frank is the opposite end of that.

What was cool is it was one of the first gigs where I came in and did my thing, bringing that big energy to these fuckin' heavy industrial songs. I don't think Gary gave me any notes; he just let me do my thing. And it was cool to hear the fans say how much they really enjoyed the energy I brought to that first show at the cemetery. Danny Lohner from Nine Inch Nails was there with Alkaline Trio's Matt Skiba, and I remember seeing them at the afterparty. They both were like, "Dude, the fucking energy you bring to this band and everything is next level." And it's cool to get respect from those guys, you know?

I've had so many amazing moments with all these legends I've had the opportunity to play with. I just go and do my thing and it's all I know. And I love that. To have those moments with these legends has been really special throughout my career, which just proves again, I'm on the right path, and I'm doing what I need to be doing.

5
THE SUM OF ALL THE PARTS

So, if you're still keeping up with me, I immediately went straight from Dhani and thenewno2 to Scott Weiland, and then back to the Street Drum Corps Vegas residency at the Hard Rock. Then during that Vegas residency, I went out and toured with Gary Numan. It was during that time, while I was touring with Gary and maintaining the Vegas gig, that Steve "Stevo" Jocz left Sum 41.

That's how it started.

The first time I saw Sum 41 play was when Street Drum Corps were out on the 2007 Warped Tour. I had never seen a band command a crowd like that and deliver such a powerful performance. I was blown away! *Chuck* is easily one of my favorite records of all time. Years later (2013), Deryck Whibley joined SDC for the opening night of our Las Vegas residency. This is the first time we ever performed together, and to feel the energy coming off him was something magical. We actually performed an early version of "There Will Be Blood," which was released on Sum 41's *13 Voices* record years later. Around this same time, I opened up Facebook and I saw a post from Stevo announcing he's quitting the band. I immediately emailed Deryck to say, "Sorry that you just lost a brother from the band. Whenever you're ready, please give me an opportunity because I've always wanted to be in this band, and I will deliver."

The only time I ever got calls from multiple concerned people was when I was going to play for Scott Weiland. Adrian Young, who played on his record, called me. Adrian's wife used to be in one of Scott's production teams for a bit back in the day. Chester called me because he was doing the STP thing.

The only person who genuinely seemed concerned about Sum 41 was my wife, Lauren. When I told her, "Hey, I'm jamming with Deryck" and whatnot—she had gone to a couple of parties at Deryck's house and saw him in Vegas—she was just like, "I don't think he's in a good place right now. Like, are you sure?" And I'm like, "Let's just see where this goes," which is completely natural. Besides, there was nothing really happening with the band after touring behind *Screaming Bloody Murder*, anyway. I'm just exploring this opportunity. That was really it.

Nobody else in the industry, you know, even to this day, calls Deryck "*That* fuckin' guy" or whatever. The only people that'll talk shit on Sum 41 are probably bus companies, hotels, and venues from back in the early 2000s that the band destroyed from partying. You know, funnily enough, our bus driver on this last European tour drove them years prior. He was the driver who had to pull the bus over because they were going crazy, throwing potato chips and smashing glasses on the bus, so he freaked out on them. Fast forward to 2024, and he's driving us again, and we're having hot tea and going to bed early. That's pretty funny...

My first US tour with Sum 41 was the 2016 Warped Tour. I had only done Warped with SDC, where we had to build our own stage. In the following years, they put us in a tent and at the top of a skate ramp. I had never played on a proper stage there. I remember playing one of the first shows with Sum on the Warped mainstage, and Kevin Lyman is right behind me as I'm playing.

I get off stage, and he goes, "This is what the Warped Tour is about. You started this tour building your own stage, now you're headlining the mainstage. You paid your dues. Congratulations." And that was the most amazing thing someone's ever said to me. He gets it. He's in the position he's in because he built it just like I did, you know? Kevin's been such a key component of my life. He's just somebody that I looked up to so much that I wanted to get that respect from him. He was right: I started out in the parking lot and then I'm on the fucking mainstage because I stayed on the path and just kept going and going. It's a great story that really sums up how I feel about my life and my mission.

Then fast-forward to the final Warped Tour when they did two shows in Jersey and two shows at Shoreline Amphitheater in Mountain View, California. Sum 41 is one of the headliners on the mainstage, and Street Drum Corps gets to open the amphitheater stage for the day. Now SDC is finally on a real stage, many years later. I go play the set with Sum 41 directly afterward. The Used asks SDC to join them onstage, so there I was, onstage with a marching snare drum, making music with the Used and Street Drum Corps. I get off stage from The Used's set to do a workshop at the SJC Drums booth. I'm jamming with young drummers that won a contest to play with me at this little intimate workshop. I'm thinking about all the shows and sets I've played, and I think I'm done for the day.

Our manager comes on our bus. "NOFX is going to be really late." They're the headliner tonight for the "final-ever" Warped Tour date.

"Their flights are canceled. So they're flying privately, but they're not going to get here in time. They want you guys to go up and start the set, and then they'll just run in." So Sum learned NOFX's "Stickin in My Eye" and filled in for them until they showed up. I opened the day, and I closed the day. What a way to celebrate everything I've built in one place.

Anyway, back to my Sum 41 origin story: Deryck and I started this whole journey by jamming and recording drums, as he was starting to write again and was also dialing in his home studio. I didn't know if there was going to *be* a Sum 41 since the band wasn't really together and Deryck was recovering. I was there as a friend whenever he called or needed me.

Before he collapsed and wound up in the hospital, we had started jamming for fun at his house. By then, I was dealing with all the prep for my wedding. I invited Deryck and I didn't hear back from him. When I got home from my honeymoon, he reached out. He said, "Sorry I didn't respond about your wedding. This is what happened to me. I'm in the hospital. I'm going to be home soon." So I went and visited him and just sat with him for hours at his house as he told me everything that happened. He mentioned that Dave Brownsound had just visited him only days prior to me being there, and he was thinking about the band, saying he would love to be in Sum again. That was really exciting.

We started as he was recovering. Deryck was experimenting in his home studio with various drum sounds and new recording gear. I would come over, and we would put the drums in his living room, and then in other rooms, we were just testing the tones and trying to capture the right drum sound. It was important to be there for him when he was getting inspired to be in the studio again and writing music. We were recording the song "There Will Be Blood" that he played when he guested with Street Drum Corps during the Vegas residency.

Deryck said he was talking to Cone [McCaslin, Sum bassist] and Tom [Thacker] again. They both came to LA, and we jammed for a week straight. They would say, "Learn these songs today." We'd go through them, and then other batches, day after day. I mean, we worked through the catalog and deep cuts, too.

He put together a band with his friends and me, and we started doing pop-up shows all over SoCal. The reasons were two-fold: First, he needed to get back onstage. And second, he wanted to break me in by working together. The band was called Deryck Whibley and the Happiness Machines. We played the Lyric Theatre in LA, and Mikey Way from My Chemical Romance joined us on bass for "In Too Deep." His brother Gerard and guitarist Ray Toro were there too and everyone was freaking out. We played a Sum 41 set and some covers. It was great seeing Deryck getting back onstage again and us working together.

After that, that's when the whole band started rehearsing and getting ready for the APMAS award show in Cleveland. Dave was back in the band, but we kept it a secret until the night of the show. There was a lot of covert stuff going on leading up to that AP show. We were also secretly making the *13 Voices* record.

But here's the thing: I've always been a hired gun in every other band, right? Sum 41 was the first time where I was actually in a real band at this level with that kind of success. It was the golden ticket for me. It was special because I was given an opportunity where nobody else was auditioned or anything like that. Street Drum Corps was still thriving. It's not like I quit everything to do this. I still had a company that I was the CEO of.

I was down to give Sum 41 a ride. We kept touring. That was the longest touring I'd ever done with the band—nine straight weeks in Europe on that first cycle. It was a long, non-stop cycle. After that, we were supposed to be in the studio writing a record. Instead, we went on tour for the anniversary of *Does This Look Infected?* We then wrote and recorded *Order In Decline* and then started that tour cycle. Right in the middle of that campaign, COVID hit. It all shut down for a good year until Deryck started writing again, and then he and I were in the studio recording and doing pre-production. It all started back up and went until the final tour.

For me, the story of me joining Sum 41 is about seeing something that you really want, putting yourself out there, going for it, and getting that gig before they even do auditions. They had *everybody* calling them! I just had that relationship with them and let it be known right away—in a respectful manner—that whenever they were willing to jam, I wanted an opportunity. It's a band that I always loved, and I just knew it would fit my style. Everything would work, and I pursued something in a respectable way. That's what I talk about to the kids in my workshop too when they ask, "How'd you get in Sum 41?" I'm like, "There's a lesson here. I wasn't annoying about it. I didn't go through management. I just went right to Deryck, sent him a very nice email, and here I am, fucking ten years later."

Actually, the way I found out I was in the band was kind of funny. They were doing a photo shoot in Deryck's garage because they had some shows coming up. I was there, but I just walked the other way, because I didn't know if I was in the band. *Maybe I'm not going to play on the records, and I'll just play live.* You know how it is. When you replace a big member, you're just the hired gun. So that's what I had preconceived in my own head. And then they go, "Hey Frank, jump in the photo. You're in the band."

DERYCK WHIBLEY, frontman/guitarist/founding member of Sum 41:
Frank's one of those guys that knows everybody and he's always around. I'd seen him around a few times before we actually met. I think once we actually

had a conversation, we were introduced by Tommy Lee, and it would have been backstage at a Mötley Crüe show. But we'd sort of run in circles where I'd bumped into him and kind of recognized him a few times through Warped Tour and stuff like that.

When Stevo left the band, Sum was in a really bad place. We were kind of imploding, personally and professionally, and my drinking was out of control. Everything was just falling apart at that point, right? So when Stevo left, there wasn't really much of a band left. I wasn't thinking about music anymore.

I wanted to just take a break from it, and you know, as soon as Stevo announced publicly that he had left the band, I think it was only a week later that I got an email from Zummo. I see the name "Frank Zummo" pop up in my inbox and I'm like. "I know that name, but I don't know who that is." He was like, "Hey, I heard you had a member leave, and I'd love to try out." I remember thinking, "Try-out? I'm not even thinking about the band at all." Then I thought, "OK, noted. Whenever that day comes, I'll remember Zummo."

When I started to think about the band again, I wasn't thinking of "Let's get somebody to play on the record, then we'll figure out a drummer to just come in and be part of the gang with us." We're all going to be on a tour bus together; we're not going to hire somebody for the record, and then hire somebody else for the show like this—we're bringing somebody into the family. Zummo and I just started hanging out first, just to see what we were like as friends before we even played any music. We did that for a while.

We got along pretty well right away. Frank was excited to play with somebody who was into music, as I was into someone who's truly interested in playing drums. And that's not a diss to Stevo—he'd always talk publicly about how he hated recording, hated playing drums, and never practiced. It was something he could do, and he liked being in a band, but he didn't care for all the other stuff. So here comes a drummer who's like, "I love playing drums, let's work on music. Let's do (all the other) stuff." And I'm like, "Wait, this is so much different than what I'm used to."

As I was going downhill, my last year of drinking was the worst. That's what led me into the hospital. But during the last six months of my drinking, Zummo and I were hanging out. We were trying to talk about music, and I was still trying to be productive, even though I was being destructive at the same time. I spent about a month in the hospital and I couldn't do anything, always hooked up to all these IVs and wires and all this stuff. But I was sober. And all I could think about was playing music and just getting out and back into it.

Zummo and I started talking about the future. I was trying to write again and just get back into it. I'd have Zummo come over to the house and jam on little bits of ideas that I had and it progressively grew. Even at that point though, we'd never said he was the drummer. We never really said, "OK, this is it. We're going to make a record. We're gonna do this." We were just still kind of growing as friends. Then I got to a point where I had a few songs that were almost done, and even though he still wasn't officially in the band, I said, "Hey man, I'm gonna go to the studio. Do you want to play some drums on this stuff?" It was another "let's test it out in the studio before we make any commitments" and still feeling each other out. But it was incredible. Like I've said in the past—and this is very public—Steve always hated playing in the studio. It was not his cup of tea, *at all*. So to have the opposite—somebody who was so genuinely excited to be in the studio—was just really fun and refreshing. That totally blew my mind. I was like, "He's gotta be the guy."

The other guys hadn't met him yet and didn't really know much about Zummo. They'd never met him, so I had to say, "Hey, I've been working with this guy, Frank Zummo—and he's *really* good." And they're like, "OK, who is he? What's going on?" Because I think in their minds, they thought Stevo might come back. "You guys gotta come down to LA and meet this guy!"

Tom, our guitar player, was in New York at the time, and Cone was in Toronto. Brownsound was still in Toronto, but he was not back in the band yet. We were still kind of putting the pieces together. So it was really just Cone and Tom. And I was like, "You guys have got to come down. Let's jam." They came down, we jammed, and they were like, "Wow, we like this guy. He's different than Stevo, but not in a bad way. They're totally different drummers, but what an interesting feel, what a vibe!" There it was: It just felt new and different, but in a really good way. Not better… it's like they're not better or worse, they're just different. You know, we'd been a band for a long time, and then there was talk of Dave coming back in. It was starting to feel like a new band. So it made sense, you know, to feel different.

I consider Zummo a great friend, regardless of his drumming. I mean, he's awesome on tour, easy to talk to, and he's got solid touring etiquette. Frank's not what we call on tour, "a punisher." He's an easy-going, fun-to-hang-out-with kind of guy. He was over here last week with his kids on Easter, and our kids were having an Easter egg hunt together. Frank feels like family.

The thing that always stands out to me is when I had the idea that *Heaven and Hell* was going to be the last Sum record and the last tour, I would say Frank was the person I worried about the *least* regarding what he was going to do next.

Just because of his work ethic, who he is, and how great he is. That's what I think about when I think of Frank. He's the kind of guy that will always make something remarkable happen for himself.

Deryck's the one who told me in the beginning, "We always have to prove ourselves." We always had to deal with past agents saying, "We've got to build the band back up, guys. We've got to take this tour. We've got to go play these underplays," whatever it is. One of my SDC group-managers at one point was Paul Pontius. He was an A&R rep for Sum 41 during their heyday on Island/Def Jam. He told me nothing but great things about the guys. It was never anything that was alarming, you know? So all that stuff was like, "OK well, cool." Now we've got a lot to prove. Got a new drummer. Got a new record, as well. Deryck is sober now. *Bring it on. Let's do this.*

The musical bond that the five of us create and put out there is powerful… And we're so spoiled by how crazy our fans go. I can't imagine it never feeling like that again. It's easy playing an amazing show because the audience is just right there with you, fully engaged. But then I've played with some artists like Gary Numan where the audience is just looking at you. That's because everyone is so obsessed with Gary and he's an icon. It happened a lot with Dhani Harrison because of who his dad was, and you just have people just staring at you. There isn't anything wrong with that because that kind of music is different.

But I'm just so spoiled playing and having people go fucking nuts. When they don't, it feels almost awkward, like they're staring at you instead of just losing themselves in their own emotion and jumping around. I feel like I'm on display. Just a different energy and a different vibe.

I remember walking off stage at one of these massive festivals we did this past summer in Europe and saying to Deryck, "Wouldn't that be weird if we didn't feel that again? It would be weird because we're so spoiled. Our fans are so great. To go on stage and not feel that again? That would be tough, you know?"

6
OBEY!

I've always been a fan of Shepard Fairey's work. I love art, and what I love most about Shepard's art is how he presents political concepts in a beautiful way while getting the point across. I love the punk-rock upbringing that's reflected in his art. And you know, when I was a kid, I used to go see Andre the Giant wrestle back in the day. So when I started seeing those iconic Andre "OBEY" stickers all over New York, it was like a mystery, like "what is this?" Once I found out what it was and who this man was (and everything he stood for), I became a fan.

I met Shepard early on when Street Drum Corps started. We both performed at an MTV Video Music Awards pre-kickoff event up in the Hollywood Hills. Shepard was DJing, and Street Drum Corps was doing our little drum performance, so I introduced myself to him. Then years later, when I started playing with Dhani Harrison, he and Dhani were good friends, and Shepard was coming around a lot. We became friends.

After a movie premiere event thenewno2 played in support of the *Beautiful Creatures* film, Shepard and I were hanging out backstage at Henson Recording Studios. I was performing with thenewno2 the next day on *The Tonight Show*. And I was like, "Wow, Shepard. I've got a beautiful white drum kit. How sick would it be for you to paint this drum kit for Leno tomorrow?" And he's like, "Well, I obviously can't do this in time, but how about I paint your bass drum head?" I asked him if he had done that before, and he said no. "I'd never done that. I've done a lot of album covers and posters for bands, but I've never painted drums." So he painted mine: a striking thenewno2 drumhead that I performed with on the Jay Leno show. When Street Drum Corps got our residency in Las Vegas, Shepard painted my kick drum head for the duration. After the residency, the drum went into their memorabilia display in the casino.

The goal was always to one day have Shepard paint a drum kit of mine. At my wedding, instead of Lauren having some guest book that everyone signs and then we toss it in a drawer and never see again, we actually got a kick drum. We had it on an easel where everyone who walked into our wedding signed it and left well wishes. To this day, I have it in my studio, where I look at it every day. Shepard painted the drum head as a wedding present, and it remains very special to us.

When I joined Sum 41, we were on the Warped Tour. And on Warped, there's no dressing rooms, and you're stuck on your bus all day, all night. It seemed like the news was always on in the bus, and every time I would glance at the TV, I just saw all this horrible gun violence happening. It was time to design a drum kit for the Sum 41 World Tour, my first album cycle with the band. I called Shepard and told him it felt like now's the time for him to paint a drum set or design a kit for me. "I'm seeing all of this appalling gun violence happening with children, just mass shootings and all this terrible stuff." And Shepard goes, "I have this piece called *Rise Above*. It's a beautiful mandala, but if you look closely, it's all pieces of defragmented gun parts." I looked at the piece. It was beautiful. SJC Drums figured out how to put his art on the drums. They actually etched the mandala onto them so you can feel all the gun parts and everything on the drum surface.

And this is how I speak politically: I communicate through my art. I don't run my mouth on social media and interviews to rant about it. This drum kit really expressed what I was feeling about this rampant gun violence. It's done in that beautiful way Shepard creates art, and it meant something every time I played it. Now it's on display at the Hard Rock Las Vegas for everyone to enjoy and see. Since then, we've made multiple drum kits together, special pieces that we've raised for charity and music schools.

Shepard has become such a dear friend and unwavering supporter, and he said some really incredible things about me that are just so special coming from someone I respect so much.

SHEPARD FAIREY, artist, activist, and founder of Obey Clothing: I love Frank. We've been friends for a long time. I'm not super-tight with Frank, but we've collaborated a bunch. I've collaborated with him, socialized with him, and paid attention to all the projects he does. I feel like there's this natural overlap because we have a lot of similar tastes and overlapping friend circles, so it was like whether I wanted to or not, Frank Zummo was going to be in my life. I'm so glad that he's such a nice guy because, yeah, I might have to bail on a lot of stuff I'd normally want to do if I didn't like him.

I met Frank through Bobby Alt. When Bobby was in S.T.U.N., I liked their music and invited S.T.U.N. to be part of an anti-George Bush rally we held called Be the Revolution in 2000 and the summer of 2004. Then Bobby told me about Street Drum Corps, and I met Frank shortly thereafter. I don't know exactly when Street Drum Corps was formed, but I know I've known Frank for about 20 years.

I've painted two different kits for Frank: one for Street Drum Corps and then two more since he's been in Sum 41, and then we also worked on a collaboration with SJC Drums where I did the design, and it was something they produced based on a digital file. That's at least four different projects we've done together involving Frank's drums. It's always an honor that Frank's so psyched on my artwork and wants to collaborate. And he's such a phenomenal drummer, and I know it means a lot to have my work on his drums. It's just not always practical. Painting an entire drum kit by hand is actually pretty time-consuming.

One thing you'll know about Frank, I'm sure, is that he's an irrepressible force of nature who is totally enthusiastic about everything he's doing. I'm almost always wanting to say "yes" because I want to be part of that infectious, positive energy he brings. But it's not all doable sometimes. In a nutshell: Frank represents what I want to see in the world. He believes in creative self-determination through hard work; never accepting "that's impossible" as an answer; and always giving back. He does all these drum workshops where he sees in these kids the possibility of the spark he felt as a kid discovering drums, with his dad being a drummer. It's extremely moving stuff. (So you know: On the inside, I'm a total bleeding heart, and then on the exterior, I wear skull shirts and I'm trying to be cool.) But when I see somebody who's got a similar thing going on, it's meaningful to me, and Frank has that.

I can't speak for Frank because we've never had a deep conversation about this exact idea. I think having learned art and design in the analog era (where everything was an uphill slog in the snow both ways), but then learning how to use the computer has made me able to take that "by any means necessary" mindset and use better tools. I think that growing up on the East Coast and everything being a struggle, having to dig your heels in for your beliefs and being resourceful allowed us to harness whatever sort of ragtag community we could assemble to support each other. Having that and then coming to the West Coast, where there's a bit more of a hippie spirit and a creatively fertile landscape? I think you've got the best of both worlds. I feel extremely lucky in that capacity, that I have my work ethic from the East Coast merged with the more laid-back culture of the West Coast. There's a reason why I'm very committed to living in California. Frank has moved to NorCal to get some space and serenity, but he feeds off the culture and energy of not only California but also of all these places he travels to while on the road.

I see it as maybe the California mentality or the California culture helping people find a rhythm between that super-intensity and the necessary recharge for a sustained career. I tend to be easily overstimulated and overcommitted—and I get that sense from Frank, too. I don't know; I can't speak for him. But I think the "me and my small group of friends against the world" mentality serves you really well when you're in a certain phase of your career, by the virtue of "hey, we're all in this together," which is more of a California approach. You could call it punk-rock DIY mixed with a bit of hippie compassion.

Another thing I like about him is that Frank doesn't make excuses, *ever*. For him, it's like the bump in the road is just a chance to evolve, pivot, adapt. *What did we learn from that?* I don't know what's up with his brain chemistry that he embraces everything like that. It's this relentless force of "OK, there's a setback. But I'm going to keep going and it's going to work out." And when you have that mentality, it generally does manifest if you're a hard worker. I absolutely believe in that myself, but I do hit moments of disillusionment here and there. I think Frank's maybe more of a perpetual optimist than I am, and I really admire that about him. We haven't had a long discussion about his next phase that he's entering now, but he's already got his next projects going. I think he just doesn't stop moving.

I think some people, once they've established themselves as a major force in whatever category they're in, see themselves as competitors against people who came before them but are still performing at a high level (like Tommy Lee) and aren't particularly reverent. But Frank is different; he's like, "I get to be Frank Zummo over here," as his own distinct entity who's been celebrated in drum magazines and websites all around the globe. But then, he'll step in as the temporary drummer in Mötley Crüe and be genuinely grateful for that opportunity. And that's cool. That self-confidence mixed with reverence for his influences? Yeah, not enough people have that. Frank has shown that you can have your own identity and inner security without being a petty competitor. There are so many people who do great things, yet I see how they act like prima donnas about stuff. Man, that's so sad. You're in the upper stratosphere of whatever field you're in, and you're acting like this towards other people. Frank is good to people.

A lot of folks neglect the thing that brought them some notoriety in favor of just being "me, me, me." Frank is constantly dedicated to the art of drumming, and when I watch the raw energy that goes into it... How many calories is he burning with the kind of relentless cardio he's getting? He's got so much energy because he's so friggin' disciplined about staying in great shape to maintain that endurance. Naturally, as we age, some of that energy becomes harder to sustain. But for where he is now, there's absolutely no sign of him losing steam and slowing down—except maybe that he's chosen to have a bit more peace and quiet with his family life when he's not out on the road. But I'm sure he's drumming for four hours a day at home, anyway.

At one point, Frank knew that I liked Queens of the Stone Age. He invited me and my wife to see them in Vegas when we were unveiling one of the drum kits at the Hard Rock. He was super excited about how he organized the press event for the drum kit, us going to see Queens, and us saying what's-up to the band. To me, it's sort of like Frank's recognizing this cultural ecosystem that's meant a lot to both of us, so we can share it.

Frank's comfortable interacting with *anyone*. When he was drumming for thenewno2 and you have Dhani Harrison—George Harrison's son—as the leader of the band, and you've got iconic figures like Annie Lennox and Jeff Lynne from ELO and Ringo Starr all coming around… Frank can casually hang with any of those people and not seem either disrespectfully blasé or like a sycophant. He just knows how to roll.

I think whether you've had mental health struggles or whether you know what's worked for you (because you naturally have a more positive brain chemistry and you've been able to manifest the things that genuinely excite you), everybody's had some failures and setbacks that they had to recover from. I think Frank is very sympathetic to how not everyone is maybe automatically as resilient from failure and as self-confident as he is. The whole What's on Your Plate exercise of writing this stuff on the two sides of a paper plate… I don't know whether he's been coached on that as a technique to get people to come out of their shell and then also think about their goals. That's a truly beautiful thing, and you know he's not making big bucks doing it. Maybe he's doing it out of a sense of how to give back or how to build a world he would rather live in.

When people say to me, "You do so much stuff for charity, it's so selfless," I go, "Great that you're giving me some credit here. But if I may be a contrarian, I could also say it's very selfish because when I look at all the meanness in the world, all the selfishness, all the racism, sexism, xenophobia, I very selfishly want a world I'd rather live in without that stuff." So I don't know what's driving Frank. But he's doing it…

Frank is really relentless in pursuit of what he wants to do. He always stops short of being somebody that's irritating to me. I do get a chuckle out of his dogged persistence; I think he's really someone who's figured out a way to balance being ambitious without being obnoxious. I've got to give him a lot of credit for that, because there are a lot of people who are too timid and they don't accomplish anything, or they're just so self-absorbed, they're oblivious to how they just steamroll other people. And I think Frank gets the balance right.

I will say that because he's so energetic, it can be exhausting keeping up with Frank. Say when we're doing a video shoot for SJC Drums at my studio or we're doing a thing at the Hard Rock, he's going to try to maximize every media opportunity and every relationship for a great experience. "Oh yeah, my friend's gonna take you up to the Hard Rock archive, and we can take some photos up there." And at first I'm thinking, "Oh God, another thing to do." Then it ends up being awesome because my wife gets to put on the jacket that Iggy Pop sported on the cover of *The Idiot*. I think it's going to be another thing where I'm like, "I'm so fatigued," but then it ends up being totally worth it.

It makes sense: Frank is the quintessential "lust for life" guy.

7
RUDIMENTS... AND RUDE AWAKENINGS

I often get asked about getting started and rudiments at the workshops. So here is my straightforward guide for players, from starting out to the pro level. First, go buy a practice pad and get two books: *Stick Control* by George Lawrence Stone and *Syncopation*. These are foundational materials every drummer should work on. They are incredible for your coordination, your chops, your hands—all of that—going through those patterns and stickings. You don't have to know how to read music to do it: It's just like right, left, in various configurations. *Syncopation* starts easy, focusing on reading, then it gets more challenging as you go through the book. But just sitting down with a pad and working through those two books is really what shaped me. I still refer back to them and work through those routines. That's for beginners who want to start reading.

Next, start working on technique. I'm a double-bass drummer. I started very young, and my first drum kit had two kick drums. I grew up in that era, and I still play two kick drums because not only is it natural to me, but I also play in bands that have double-bass parts. I feel like I have more power with the two kick drums. There's a book by Joe Franco called *Double Bass Drumming*. It features all these great rhythms using double bass. I learned from that book and when I was teaching, I would introduce it to anyone who wanted to learn double bass. It's a fun book and really great for developing your beat coordination in the double-bass world. There are obviously other great books for single-foot players if you're not a double-bass player.

There are a ton of books for all kinds of drumming techniques. What I tell every person just starting is that the first thing you should do is go put on your favorite music, your go-to YouTube videos or Spotify playlists. (That's what my kids do and I don't even tell them to do that, which is awesome.) Just go and have some self-discovery! You might not know what you're doing, just like my dad gave me his record collection and speakers and told me to "have at it." I had years of self-discovery before I took lessons. *I didn't know what I was doing.* I was just figuring it out to Led Zeppelin and James Brown, Sly And The Family Stone, AC/DC, Queen, and then later, the Mötley Crües and Ozzys. I didn't know what I was doing, but it was so fun because I was just wilding out, exploring, and discovering all this stuff that was foreign to me. I always say that self-discovery is vital because, just like those books I mentioned, playing to records helps you build tempo. As drummers, we want to have good tempo. Everyone wants to be in a band with someone who has good tempo. Even if you're a YouTube drummer, you're playing along to songs that have been recorded to click tracks. I feel like that's why I have such a good tempo. Because I played to records forever, then that turned into cassette tapes, then CDs, then MP3s. So that really helps.

Then, obviously, you should get a traditional metronome. You can get an app (some are free) and just go through all different tempos, from slow to fast. Stay on it until you don't even notice you're playing to that BPM anymore because you're just one with it. I only hear the count-in of a song, and then I don't hear the click anymore because we're best friends now. We are one. I don't even notice it: I just hear the four or eight count to start something, and then it fades away because I'm just so naturally accustomed to it.

So: my warm-up. I start with 120 BPM until I feel good. Then I go up by 10 BPM until I hit 180. After 180, I'm done and move on to the next thing. But I'll spend a good three to five minutes as part of my warm-up going through each one of those tempos. When I was a kid, I'd pick one tempo, and that would be my tempo for the day. And I would just jam, jam—play simple beats, hard fills, and try to make sure I was landing back on the one again. So play to a click track, practice self-discovery, which can be any form you want it to be, the book stuff... And then obviously, we live in a world now where we have access to everything on the YouTubes and the Drumeos—all these great places where you can watch your favorite drummer dissect their parts, explain how they made it, how it sounds, and how you can play it. There's so much free stuff out there that whatever you're into, you can dive down a rabbit hole and find all this amazing content to really learn from. Sometimes even the guys in my band will pull out a deep cut they forgot how to play or aren't sure about because it's hard to make out the recording. Usually, there's some guy who made a tutorial, and he's showing you how to do it. And most of the time, they're spot-on.

I highly recommend all that stuff. And then I suggest enrolling in a place like School of Rock where you have your one-on-one lessons at your instrument, but then you also get to play with other musicians and experience that. At School of Rock, you learn how to be professional for a gig and what it takes to do a gig, from showing up on time to soundchecking to learning a set of music to being onstage at a certain time and offstage at the end. All this stuff you get to learn is pretty incredible.

And you're playing covers. You're learning from the Beatles, from Metallica—so this is a great path for just starting out. For drummers who are well into their career, I would also stress that you can find someone there to help you with proper technique. You don't want to learn how to play the wrong way because it can hurt you, and hitting drums and things incorrectly is just not healthy. I was lucky enough early on to go to a teacher who helped correct all of my imperfections, which is why I'm still able to do it at this point. Even when I checked in with Dave Elitch after COVID, we focused on other stuff because times have changed since I had my last technique teachings (like sports and training), and instructors find new ways. It's like a constant evolution of learning, so you definitely wanna get with someone who can look over your playing—the way you're hitting the drums, the way you're kicking the pedals, where your posture is—all that stuff.

Also: Stay physically in shape. You gotta be an athlete, so your health routine is crucial. Consider what you're eating and how your health is. Even if you're a kid and you're riding your bike every day, that's great, but now get off your bike and go play drums! Watch what you're eating and putting into your body. Stay away from all the garbage. It's hard for kids: My kids are really healthy, but when Halloween rolls around and all the candy comes out, they go nuts. And most of the time, it's the most garbage, chemical-laden junk. Obviously, everything in moderation...

Yes, drumming sounds like a lot of work. It *is* a lot of work, and it's a big commitment. But so is everything in life. You get a puppy, and it's a huge commitment to train that dog and take care of it. I mean, success requires work and dedication, and music is at that level—if this is what you're truly passionate about. And what I always say is, if this is what you want to do, just do it until it happens. Like tunnel vision: *This is what I want to do, and I'm going to go and work on every single aspect of it.* Then, when you reach a certain level, it becomes a business: *How am I going to put myself out there? Am I going to put myself out there on social media? Am I going to get into a band? How are we going to start working with the band?* It's a whole process.

It pays off if you put the work in. You know, I sacrificed a lot. I didn't really do sports or a lot of social activities because I was just so *driven.* I was just happy coming home from school, locking myself in the basement, and pretending I was playing arenas in these bands that I was jamming along to. That was better than anything.

The common complaints I always hear at my workshops can be summarized into these top three: "My wrist hurts," "My elbow hurts," or "I'm getting really fatigued. What should I do?" It's great that they're acknowledging that because when I was young, I didn't think about it. I just played through it. But now it's being talked about.

It all begins with the technique stuff—you know, not learning in a way where you're hitting drums the wrong way. It's not going to have good effects on your body for the long game. Today, there's YouTube. You can see videos and learn the right technique stuff from all these great drummers for free.

Something that all teachers—and even self-taught kids—are conscious of is wellness. They're going down the rabbit hole and seeing drummers talking about it. I mean, think about it: You're beating the living shit out of objects with your whole body, and of course, it can really mess you up. Just like in sports, you have to learn the right way to do it.

I get injuries from all kinds of repetitive this 'n' that. But when you do something the wrong way, you know, shit happens. The important thing is learning how not to ignore it. I tell the kids that if they are having issues, what works for me might not work for you. But there are some hacks and things I've tried, from experimenting with different supplements to perfecting techniques. Like, I'll offer a bunch of options, and then they can see which of those things their bodies respond to and go from there.

The thing that Dave Elitch worked on with me was my foot technique with striking. We tweaked some stuff with how I was striking the pedals and hitting them, which was a really cool experiment. He was like, "Go get a red Solo cup right now and smash it with your foot." I was like, OK. He's continued, "The way you just smashed it, that's how you need to hit your pedals. You know, so many people play their pedals, like it's always the top, heel up, heel down, this, that… but it's simply about smashing the pedal, just stomping on it." Dave was also the first person to teach me about the tension on my pedals. I would just take them out of the box and put them on my drums, and they felt good. But he's like, "Bro, the way you're playing, how fast you're playing, these pedals can't keep up. You have to adjust and tighten the shit out of your spring." I did that, and all of a sudden, it was easier to play this fast.

I had new drumsticks made. They're aluminum, not wood. After the folks at Ahead Drumsticks saw me with Sum 41, they helped me create a new drumstick because I was using the wrong ones for our style. For as fast as I'm playing, the weight needs to be at a certain balance, either the butt end or the tip end of the stick, with how fast I'm whipping around and the way I throw my arms. Things have changed over time—drumsticks, pedals, foot technique, hand technique—and I'm sure there's more that I'm forgetting.

And then there's my health stuff. Last night, for example, I went straight into the ice bath straight from the stage. And I was like, "This is our third show in a row. Double the ice order for me. I need to suffer tonight." I felt like I had to turn it up a level, and the venue's hospitality team sure enough delivered! The cold plunge is something like no other: to go from that raw energy onstage and that madness to submerging yourself for three-and-a-half minutes in an ice bath of stillness and calm? It's pretty incredible. Doing that makes me drum better and helps my body heal. If you want to be at this level that I'm at, and everyone's saying, "I'm exhausted watching you, how do you do it?" It's because of all these techniques, all this training, getting proper sleep, controlling what food and beverages go into my body, and what my training is for the day. It's dedication to the craft at its most extreme, and I absolutely love it. Acting like an idiot on tour and being a maniac while not being healthy is not an option.

When I started touring fully with Sum, there weren't any breaks. I was going from Sum to Krewella to whatever else I was doing—just nonstop. And I had a shoulder problem so bad that it hurt to fucking hit the drums, you know? That was before I was taking any kind of supplements or doing saunas or ice baths. My wife discovered this company called Organixx that makes a turmeric supplement that helps with inflammation, so I got on that. Then I started working with a massage/bodywork guy who still works on Deryck and me to this day. He got in there and broke up all the scar tissue from all that inflammation.

Lately, everything's been OK. There have been little things here and there, but I dealt with them right away. Like this summer, I woke up one day and my back was just... something wasn't right. Every step I took hurt really bad. I went to somebody to work on it, and they showed me a bunch of different stretches, and it was over in a day, thankfully. But then I had problems with my right foot. So this year was crazy with me juggling some solo shows, workshops, a lot of Drumheads shows, and a lot of DJ shows.

I was jumping up and fucking down so much—and jumping on concrete—that one day, something in my right foot, like my Achilles or whatever, just got tweaked. I want to say it was late September. It's still not 100%. I've been getting it worked on, but I would say it's the longest injury I've had. I just tweaked it—maybe I jumped wrong or landed wrong, not sure. It's been very frustrating because it's my main kick drum foot. I don't really feel it when I'm drumming, but walking and being reminded by this little pain that I'm not able to run is fucking crazy.

I bought one of those Rogue Echo bikes: it's not a Peloton; it's a bike where you're pulling with your hands and pedaling with your feet to power it. That didn't hurt my foot, so I was able to use it to get the cardio miles in. But it's been a fucking bummer. It's the most painful thing because I need to break up so much scar tissue in my foot to deal with it. But it's knowing *how* to deal with it and not letting the pain pile up and change things. Shit happens. The reality is that drummers are fucking athletes who don't stop, you know? It's not like there's a specific season where we stop playing.

I'm convinced that drumming beats any workout you could do, especially for your heart rate. It's the best workout *ever*. That's why, when I'm on tour, I have some weights and kettlebells and things to use backstage for strength. The cardio is playing the show. And then, on a day off, I'll go for a run and do more weight training, just to maintain that level and keep my stamina up. That's why I have to do so much cardio when we're not touring.

I feel that drumming is a constant process. It's not been entirely mastered, and I don't think you ever can. Working with Dom Famularo and The Drummer's Collective to learn all these various styles was incredibly important for me. After COVID restrictions were lifted and things were starting back up, I was going in with Dave Elitch to work on some technique. I don't have an ego about this: anyone who is truly serious about this knows when to put in the work.

When it comes to the things I had trouble learning, I think the toughest was the really fast double bass stuff—just insane tempos. They have to be locked in with the guitars to be super-tight in those certain parts where it's starting and stopping. I wouldn't even say it's about stamina or anything like that; it's about how to execute something like that really, really *cleanly*. The problem is, when you play that fast, it can sound muddy if you're not precise. I learned that by doing a lot of studio work. In the studio, you're under a microscope and you have to be so clean with everything. Especially when you're doing pop music sessions, because they don't have time to mess around. (I have Platinum record plaques for Kelly Clarkson's *Stronger* album, as well as Orianthi's "According to You" single.) That part of the industry is like a factory: producers don't have time to sit there and edit your imperfections. They want it to be perfect, move on, boom! You know, time is money and all that stuff... So I've learned a lot of that honing, but to this day, it's still not easy. I wouldn't even say it's something I've mastered.

I train and drum off the road while sticking to a regimented warmup routine. When Sum was in Europe doing our big arena run, at the start of the tour, we played flawlessly. We were playing some of the older songs because it was a bit of an anniversary for some of the older records, and I was just in the groove. It felt nearly effortless to nail those really fast tempos.

Then... I'd say by the middle to the end of the tour, it was like the fear kicked in, and then the mental side of it came into play. I was having trouble. Thankfully, nobody noticed, but it was really fucking with my head to the point where I was getting into fight-or-flight mode and would almost freeze. I'd go to execute those parts and... freeze. And it's like that... that... that fight-or-flight moment where I would freeze up, and it really ended the tour on a bad note for me mentally. And that was scary.

I came home and thought, *I've got to figure this out. What is this? Is this just fatigue? Is it mental? What is it?* So I called a lot of the coaches I know to discuss my situation. They recommended—something I never even knew was an actual occupation—a sports psychologist. I got hooked up with this guy, Dr. Lenny Wiersma. It wasn't that I physically couldn't play those parts; clearly I could. But over time, my mental state overwhelmed me, causing this freeze reaction, and he had to work with me through many sessions.

We had to really focus my thoughts. It took a lot of sessions and a ton of work. It actually segued into me speaking with a lot of athletes and trainers who work with all the big star athletes. One even trains and works with military personnel. I did a lot of work, and it was incredibly beneficial for me. It opened the door for me to go to therapy as well. So, within the course of a couple of months, I was working with a sports psychologist, a therapist, and various trainers. I had to dig into some trauma that came up and explore why and how all these things were connected. And, you know, I'm still doing work. I finally got it in check and I'm back to a comfortable place.

I've put it in context. When you're playing over 170 BPM, it's just *insane*. It's ripping double bass for a long stretch, and to do that start/stop stuff, you've got to be so locked in with the other players in the band. You know you *want* to nail it. It's constant work, and I would say it hasn't been easy. It's an ongoing battle, something that's always kind of there and back. I constantly have to practice because I know in the back of my head, we're going to pull these songs out again or I'll be in another project or something that requires it, and I need to have that... something.

I grew up as a metal kid, playing in all kinds of death-metal bands—I mean, just crazy shit. Then I moved away from that and got into more rock and four-on-the-floor electronic bands. When I got into Sum, I had to bring all that back and really work hard to get my feet back in shape. And in the ten years I've been in the band, it's something I have to stay on top of constantly. You have to be a peak performance athlete at all times. Even during the pandemic, the big concern was not knowing when we'd be able to go back on tour. So I have to constantly keep training and practicing to stay at peak-position touring level. Deryck is the same way with that too. He is constantly singing the set while training, going to vocal lessons, and doing all that to stay in top shape because you just can't check out and go on vacation. Yes, it's good to have breaks to give your body a rest (which was what all the trainers and people told me in the beginning, "Just take a break from it!"). Just step away from it. Let's do some work just talking…

I mean, it could have been a bit of fatigue, for sure. We all get fatigued from the relentless touring and nonstop shows and stuff. So there was a little bit of that. But honestly, it was mainly mental because I *could* do it physically. It's not like all of a sudden I was asked to play a guitar solo and had never played a guitar in my life. I was executing but was having difficulties. The mental side is what got in the way and blocked me. There was a disconnect from my head to my feet, and I couldn't squeak it out. I barely got it out. And nobody in the band knew; the audience didn't know. *But I fucking knew.* And it was really defeating, and like I said, it just ended the tour in a really bad way for me.

It took such a toll on me mentally, but it was one of those things where I thought, *I'm not going to let this thing win. I need to get to the root of it. I need to understand how I can work through this moving forward.* So yeah, it was a big test, definitely a kick to the ego. But I had a problem that I needed to address.

We had to really focus when those parts and certain things came up. It was about refocusing the energy mentally, focusing it on other things, not just like, "Oh, my God, are my feet going to be able to get this out? Am I going to be able to do this?" And that's when you're not able to do it—when you're tangled up in all that mental stuff

Lenny had me focus on the whole physicality of the sound. I've got a subwoofer at my feet to feel the rumble of the bass drum because we use in-ear monitors. He was training me to focus on different ways to reprogram my brain. He'd be like, "Focus on the sensation of the drums. How does it feel versus the feeling of 'I've got to get this out?'" We gained a lot of understanding of how all these elements were connected. When I brought this up to my breath coach/therapist, she said it was basically a freeze mechanism.

That goes back to another thing that would come up in my life. When I was in a heavy situation, I would freeze instead of jumping in and being reactive. For example, on that tour, we were about to soundcheck and the house crew had one of the lighting truss bars real low. My tech didn't see it, and he fucking walked right into it and smacked his head on the thing. Everybody from the crew and the stagehands ran over to aid him. And I just shut down and froze instead of rushing over—which is what you would generally do. So that's been something in my life: When I was in very difficult situations, I would freeze. I had to get to the root of why I was freezing in moments when I should be reacting and helping? And it came back to some childhood trauma and certain situations where there would be family arguments or certain things that were unsettling for me. I would shut down, and it felt like going back to that. I did a lot of work on not having that reaction and, in these situations, fostering a more connected response instead of a shut-down response.

All of this has been great work that I've been doing over the last year, just understanding and learning how to react better and how to deal with things more effectively. And it's *definitely* a work in progress, for sure. But you know, everything is all connected in some way. This kind of drum issue opened the door to a lot of other stuff that has actually been really freeing, helpful, and therapeutic in the last year.

It's pretty amazing to uncover this stuff this late in life. I have a whole new outlook on things. I think it's helping me be a better human, partner, and father—like all this stuff. It's funny how one little thing triggered me and sent me down this whole spiral. And I'm really blessed to have these people that I can count on and talk with to understand things better. I've always been like, "It's OK, just push it aside and move on." Now I'm actually understanding a lot more, diving deeper into certain things, and just being way more in tune with everything that goes on in my life.

And in this process, this one thing that came up... The one thing that always comes up is the same comment everyone has always been saying: "You're a fucking machine." And you know, yeah, that's a good thing because it shows my hustle and work ethic. But it's also been a problem because the machine needs to chill the fuck out at certain times. Especially when I come home and I'm off the road, I've got to be present for my wife and kids. I walk in the door from the tour, and the house is in disarray because I've been on the road; there are two young kids here, and my wife's trying to do it all by herself. And I'm stressed out because the house isn't up to the standard I'd like it to be. There's laundry piled up, and it just stresses me out even though it shouldn't. Then I'm like, "For me to be comfortable in my own house, I've got to do this laundry, I've got to get these dishes put away. I've got to clean this stuff." And the reality is that's not important. I'm home for two days: My kids need me. My wife needs me here. And I'm upset or just thinking, "Go, go, go, go. Got to get the house in order so it's clean before I leave; it'll make it easier on my wife." It's about learning to just stop all that. Because that's not the bigger picture, not what's truly important. I used to come home like a fucking train: barreling through and then boom! out again. I'm re-processing all of that shit, you know? And funny enough, through this drumming issue that came up, all of a sudden I went down a rabbit hole and uncovered all this other stuff.

And honestly? I think I'll never be done working on stuff. I don't do scheduled weekly sessions. When I start feeling there's too much on my plate, I set up a session. Now, I can acknowledge it instead of just brushing it off like, "It's all good, just fucking power through." It's about being more in tune with understanding when I need help and when the plates are getting full. It's been really, really good for my family, my wife, and even the bands I'm in.

It's been a very helpful thing to uncover and dive into. I've even started talking to my mom about some stuff from the past. I had a great childhood and a healthy upbringing. But there were things that happened, and I'm acknowledging them; it's just healthy. It really is. I was one of those people that was never into sitting on a couch with a shrink or any of that kind of stuff. It just wasn't my thing. But I'm comfortable with that now because there are people that I'm comfortable with who aren't strangers. I didn't go to some corporate health provider and get assigned a shrink and I'm on the couch and all that—never felt comfortable. But this is working for me.

8
SCHOOL OF ROCK, SCHOOL OF LIFE

When it comes to career stuff—usually solo shows, DJ gigs, or one-off events—I've had managers and my team tell me, "You don't need to do this one. It's not worth your time or energy." And then I'll explore every option before making that call. But with the School of Rock workshops, everyone's like, "Go for it." There has *never* been a conversation about *not* doing a workshop. If there were, I'd probably reconsider that person being part of my team. Because if they're even thinking that, *they don't get it.*

I grew up being bullied because I was a musician and I was different. I didn't have a tribe; I didn't have School of Rock. I didn't have those supportive spaces to go to. So, because I didn't have it back then, I want to be part of it now. That's why I've gravitated to it so naturally. It's twofold: It's great to be there for these kids, to have these conversations, and to really connect. And honestly, it's also really therapeutic for me.

MIKE CIPRARI, founder of SJC Drums:

I started doing workshops in 2017. Around the NAMM trade shows, I would always pop up at Huntington Beach or one of those beaches outside Orange County to create opportunities for kids who weren't going to NAMM to meet drummers. Early on, Green Day's Tre Cool and Jay Weinberg of Suicidal Tendencies would come out, and it got bigger and bigger. I thought it'd be rad to do things like play volleyball, cook burgers on the beach, and have rock stars hanging out with kids, you know?

One year, I hit up Steve Van Doren from Vans (who I met through Kevin Lyman) and said, "Hey, I need a marker on the beach so people can see where we are. Can I borrow a Vans tent?" He gave me 10 and paid for all the food. Amazing human being. Mitch Whitaker, who at the time was the vice president of Vans, came out and was like, "What are you guys doing? This is crazy. This is so cool. How can we be more involved?" I mentioned, "In two weeks, I'm going to China with Frank Zummo from Sum 41, and we're doing a clinic tour. We're going to schools and we've got these big theaters; he's going to perform, I'm going to speak, and we'll do signings." Mitch is a drummer, so he immediately connected with this: He helped open many of the Vans Asia Pacific stores and branding. He's like, "Dude, we don't have enough time to do a lot of stuff, but let me send you some gear, and when you get back, come to my office and tell me all about it."

So we're out there in China. The music education scene over there is *waaaaay* different than it is in the States. A lot of parents want a piece of paper that says "My kid went through music-school training." Anyway, Frank and I felt like we were the Beatles while we were out there. We were being flown first-class; kids outside the venues were screaming for autographs. It was nutty, and we had a blast.

We were together every morning for breakfast and every night for dinner, both thinking, *this is cool. This is special. There's something here.* Frank—being very prepared and logistical—said, "We gotta make this a thing back home." I told him Mitch from Vans wants to meet with me when I get back from this trip and that he should come with me so we can elevate it to another level.

We ultimately ended up getting funding from Vans to do these workshops at their House of Vans venues. I got into logistical mode and leveraged my relationship with School of Rock to make it easier to book the tours. "Let's just go to all the School of Rocks. Vans will fund it, let's get in a van, and I'll bring in a couple of techs and drivers and a media person. And Frank, you do your thing: a keynote, a workshop. We'll get Vans goodies and give them to the kids." And man, we did! We put the miles on those vans, and we've flown around the country a few times. It was always an unbelievable opportunity for us to pay it forward to the kids and inspire them.

In all my years of partnering with Frank, there's never been a situation where he's said, "No, this can't be done." He'll be like, "We can do this, we *should* do this." And I'll say, "I love it, but we have this problem." And he's always like, "Great, what's the solution? Let's figure this out and make it happen." And I'm game for it. He has never turned down a challenge for the greater good. And you know, for that, I'm eternally grateful for him.

STACEY RYAN, President of School of Rock:

I met Frank through a mutual friend, Mike Cipari, founder of SJC. Mike and I started working together about 10 years ago. He has an incredible passion for inspiring youth and supporting our mission, and SJC supported our All-Stars. After a few years, he said, "Hey, I've got this great friend and partner who I think would be really good for the kids." He introduced me to Frank, and it all started there.

I don't remember exactly when my relationship with Frank started, but by the time we got hit with COVID, it was solid enough that he called me, saying, "I need to get in the schools and connect with the kids." I was like, "That's great, but we have a policy: If you're on an airplane, you can't get into a school for two weeks. You need 10 days to quarantine first." He replied, "I will drive then." And he did: He rented a car and drove to all the schools, providing inspiration at a time when everyone—our students, our community, our owners, and our staff—needed it the most.

Over the past decade, School of Rock has grown, and our brand awareness has expanded. With that said, Frank is really part of our system now. Not everyone realizes that so much of the music business is so relationship-based. And sometimes it's hard. We're for-profit, and not everyone fully understands the magnitude of what School of Rock does. So that has always been a barrier to gauging interest and generating participation. There have been incredible bands in the past—large ones like KISS, The Who, and U2—that have done incredible things with our students, and many other artists have participated as well. But Frank came right out of the gate with enthusiasm, even before experiencing it. I tell every artist, when they're getting onstage with our students for the very first time, I always tell them, "Prepare yourself; you're going to get hooked." Because the kids are great, their energy is through the roof, and there's this passion that you feel as you're doing it. Frank truly gets it. He understands the needs of our system and the needs of our students.

There hasn't been a single thing we've discussed that he's shot down or said, "No, I'm too busy." Even when he's on tour with back-to-back late-night shows, he'll still find time to engage with the School of Rock kids and do a workshop. He's been incredibly inspiring, not only because of his dedication and generosity with his time and energy, but also because the messages he shares are exactly what our kids need to hear. Rock 'n' roll isn't about drugs and alcohol and partying and staying out late. It's about exercising and eating well and taking care of your physical body and maintaining your mental health and all the things that he does to achieve that. Getting onstage and performing is his job, so his mind and body need to be able to fulfill that responsibility.

Parents have reached out to School of Rock thanking us for this partnership [with Frank]. Their comments are incredibly heartwarming. Many parents have expressed gratitude to Frank because their child feels out of place at school, not part of a group. These students see School of Rock as the only place where they truly belong. Hearing someone like Frank tell them that there will always be people who put you down, there are always going to be people that try and break you, is powerful. He discusses how to overcome those challenges and push that noise aside because it doesn't matter. There's been such incredible progress from students understanding and realizing that they're not alone. Even the coolest guy they've met to date, who's out living the dream, touring the world, playing music—you know, being a rock star—is telling them, "Yeah, people insulted me, put me down, and told me I'm no good. And that's OK, because it makes me stronger; it makes me better." That perspective helps them understand that it's part of life—not them—and teaches them how to ignore the noise.

For an impressionable youth, that messaging is so important, especially coming from someone like Frank. Just understanding that being a rebel is not a prerequisite for success in the music industry is crucial. It's not like it used to be in the old days. It now focuses on being a good human, and on being prepared, healthy, and in a position to fulfill your obligations fully and wholly while also being able to go home and live your life happily. I loved the first time I listened to Frank speak to our students. I loved everything that he had to say and knew that we needed as many of our students as possible to hear that message from him. And that's what we've been doing together for the past several years, even before COVID.

With kids these days growing up with social media, there's so much relentless noise. I'm grateful I grew up without it. I was bullied in school; I'm very tall and was called "Jolly Green Giant." I wasn't the cool kid in middle school, but to be bullied, I had to be at school or out of my house, or I'd get the random prank phone call. But for the most part, when I was home, I felt that was my safe space. Social media has created an environment where there are no safe spaces for kids these days. Online bullying is real, and it's a terrible thing, but it is reality.

School of Rock has become a big partner with SPTS, the Society for the Prevention of Teen Suicide. Frank talks about this organization at all his engagements with our school, because it's a serious problem. One life lost to suicide is one too many, so we do everything we can to educate and help kids understand that this happens, it's temporary, they're not alone, and we can get through this together. Frank's messaging and all the feedback we've received have reinforced how important our work together is and why we need to keep it going.

When it comes to the workshops, I don't plan anything. These events are organic. We *kind of* have a loose curriculum, but I don't prepare anything in advance. The kids dictate where we go and what we talk about. If I'm up there with a script, the second I do that, the kids know it's bullshit, and I lose them. Maybe it's because I'm a father now, and I just talk to my kids about everything. We have an honest, healthy relationship.

I think it's cool to have these real conversations and be there for them in that way. I didn't have anything like this growing up. I always thought clinics were boring: You'd go to a VFW hall or a drum shop, watch some dude get up there, play every fucking lick in the book that he knows, talk about every lick in that book, sign an autograph, and then leave. *Naaah.* I prefer to think of them as "events" or "workshops," and that's why we do these things at record shops, skate parks, and venues. My kids came and saw me do one of these, and they were like, "Dad, we want to go here." Now they go to School of Rock in NorCal. I didn't force them into anything; it was their choice, just like it was mine when my dad had a drum set in the house that I started playing when I was two.

The biggest takeaway is that the parents will definitely be within earshot of the meet-and-greet. There's always one who says to me, "You just sat up there and said the same thing I say, but they don't listen to me. I just saw it resonate with my kids because you said it." I'll take that.

I try to navigate the workshops as naturally as I can. If someone comes to me with a question or something that I don't know how to answer, I'm honest with them and try to steer them toward a path that could give them that knowledge. Now, obviously, I'm not a healer: You can't come to me with a problem at this event and expect me to solve it. But I will answer as honestly as I can or try to pull from my own experiences. Maybe I can point you to another resource or someone who can help. I'm definitely not a magic genie that provides you with all the solutions, but I'll try to assist as much as I can.

These kids come to me about being bullied at school, and we talk about how their parents want them to have an education. If public school isn't working out, there are alternative schools and homeschooling. We live in a world now with so many options. Your parents want you to have an education? Then find your way there—whatever that looks like for you. They're not going to say, "You can only go to public school." One dad came over to me once after hearing me talk about this, saying, "That was amazing, thank you. We're gonna explore that now."

This stuff can get really emotional. Sometimes I'm glad if I have a long drive afterward, just to take it all in and decompress. It's a lot like being a therapist. The kids open up about everything, and it's amazing to be in that position where they feel comfortable sharing. Honestly, it's just an honor to be there. I have heard stories from the School of Rock community about some teachers and kids from a few of the schools I've visited who have taken their own lives. I hope we're saving some kids and turning them around. As I said earlier, my goal with this book is to spread the word and message further than the amount of work I can do across five or six events a year.

I think it was the last day of a Loyal to the Craft workshop tour in Texas. I was jamming with this kid who was pretty young—must've been in middle school. His mom came up to me afterward and said he had been very dark, depressed, and suicidal. She was like, "When you were up there talking and performing with him, I saw this spark. Like, 'My son was *back*.' Something magical happened to him, and I had my son back." She was really emotional.

That was the first time something that powerful happened from me doing these workshops, which is pretty incredible. I was in the middle of a meet-and-greet with a couple hundred kids when she told me this, and it was so overwhelming I couldn't even process it. I told Mike from SJC, "Stop them, don't let them leave," and I went back to the line. We brought that kid out back and had some special time with him. In one of the recap videos, we presented him with a snare drum. We would bring a couple of special drums to give to kids who moved us to try to inspire them further. And that kid was fucking *beaming*. His mom was crying. And the event just set him on a new path. That's what it's about.

There've been a couple of special kids I've had performing at the workshops and whatnot, and they keep me posted constantly. Well, not *constantly*, but they'll send me videos of their drumming progress or bigger things they've done. And it's really cool that they feel like they could share that with me and want to keep me updated. I didn't have these opportunities growing up or these connections with my idols to say, "Hey, check it out. My band just played a show, here's the video." I didn't have that stuff to share with anybody besides my immediate family. So it's really cool to be in a position where these kids feel comfortable sharing that kind of stuff with me. I'm a part of their journey, and it's really, really cool.

I think the best thing a parent can do is listen to their kids. In the end, we all want our kids to be happy, get an education, be creative, and explore their passions. I always tell parents to do whatever they can to nurture that. Listening to your kids: Are they having issues or feeling unhappy? How do we get them to that place where they're thriving? As parents, we must do whatever it takes because there are so many options to get to that result. We live in a world now where there isn't just one way to reach that goal. There are fun ways to learn and to explore all these other things. And that's our mission for our kids.

If your kids aren't communicating with you and you're seeing a decline in their level of interest in education or creativity, realize that some kids aren't comfortable talking to their parents for whatever reason. Is there a family member, friend, teacher, or whoever it may be who can help and get through to them? That's why what I've been doing has been so well-received. So when the parents are like, "I tell him that a million times," I respond, "OK, great success! I'm glad I was here to reinforce something, and it resonated because I said it." So do they need that uncle or cousin or whoever to help? Too often, something tragic happens—a kid takes their own life, and the response is, "I never knew." You've got to be in tune with what's going on in their lives. What are they watching? What are they listening to? What are they seeing on social media? Because there is a rabbit hole of toxic stuff that wasn't accessible when I was a child. Back then, the only TV I watched was on Friday nights. We watched the family sitcoms, and then when I was older, the only other TV I watched was *The Headbangers Ball* and MTV because that was the only place to see the Mötley Crüe and Metallica videos I loved.

Now, we live in a world where our kids can just grab our smartphones to watch a little TV show, and they're clicking around, and before you know it, they're seeing all sorts of shit. You know, they google the wrong word or hear the wrong word, and you're all down this rabbit hole of shit. But Lauren and I communicate with our kids, as little as they are. We talk about tough things. The bottom line is *communication*. You want to have a healthy relationship with someone—your coworkers, family, friends. One thing that was instilled in my family was that if there was ever a problem, it was discussed with that person right there. It used to be, "I'm going to talk to everyone else about it, but not the person I'm pissed at." Well, who gives a shit what everybody else thinks or what they have to say? Go to the fucking source, squash it, and move on. That's how my family was.

With all the bands I play in and my personal team, it's all about communication. If I'm upset about something or whatever, I don't hold it in. I talk about it; we discuss it right there and then, and we won't let shit fester. It starts with communication. Communicate with your kids; be an open book. *Let them have that.* They should feel comfortable asking you anything or coming to you with anything because you've laid down this foundation of communication. Then you can nurture their passion, their creative pursuits, their schoolwork, you know, just whatever support you can provide. And if you see signs that things aren't working or there's a struggle, which there always are—that's life. *How do we nurture that and help them on their journey? You know, OK, maybe this isn't working, let's try something else.* I think that's the main aspect of communication—trying to get others involved if you're not getting through. So our kids can have that.

Do I care too much? Maybe… I care too much about *everything* in my life, and that's why I'm so heavily invested in anything I do. If I'm in, I'm in. You're not just getting The Part of Frank That Is Available, you know? If I set up a list of goals, I'm not stopping until all those tasks are completed. That's how I approach everything, from my notes to the lists of the year. I'm not going to stop until those things happen. Otherwise, why would I do it? Why waste my time—or anybody else's?

I've done workshops in America every year since then. Even during the pandemic, I went out and did it. And I'm always thinking, *How do we go bigger than what we've done before? How do we get more attention on this*? I've been going after big things, like doing a segment on the Fox morning show *Good Day LA* and getting a nice piece in *Forbes*. I wanna do the halftime show with the School of Rock. I'll handpick some of the kids and put together a band for that. Me and the School of Rock kids at MetLife Stadium doing a halftime show? That's the big, shooting-for-the-stars, next-level stuff I want to do. How sick would it be for these kids to play a halftime show? Those are the unforgettable experiences and amazing moments I want to create as this thing grows. I just want to see how we can go even bigger instead of continually doing what we're already doing.

The workshops are this really special thing. I've been fucking banging my head against the wall trying to explain what they are. 'Cause many people don't get it; they just think it's another freaking drum clinic. Clinics are tired flex-fests—you know, just fucking licks and talking about drum shit. My workshops are not that. I think we're finally going to get the respect they deserve and move forward. To have the anchor from *Good Day LA*—the city's biggest morning outlet—and the writer of the *Forbes* piece admit that they didn't understand it at first, but now that they do? That's simply amazing and heartwarming. Having those outlets help me spread this message is just so helpful. This is what we need; we need that word to get out.

We need to raise awareness about mental health and teen suicide prevention. It's incredible to see the acknowledgement we received this year, and I got those two huge platforms to talk about this. I can't wait to see what we're gonna do next with next year's workshops. We're already figuring things out, and now all the Schools of Rock are hitting me up personally to participate. My final workshop of 2023 was at Sweetwater in Fort Wayne, Indiana. Sweetwater has their own music school academy there. This is a completely new workshop—different everything.

This is my mantra when I'm doing the workshops: If you say you're gonna be a drummer and this is all you're going to do, don't stop until it happens. It's my livelihood, my everything. There's no reason why it can't happen. I'm fucking proof of that. I am the kid that made a pact with myself at five years old at that Mötley Crüe show. So I'm gonna do this for the rest of my life. I'm still on that path, which means working on my craft, constantly studying, practicing, learning the music business, and putting myself in situations that immerse me in the industry.

That's why I tell these kids: you see me up on these stages in front of 65,000–100,000 people, and you think it's all unattainable. *No. It is!* I'm just like you guys. Do it, and stay on that path and be the best you can be. Obviously, you have to develop a skill set, and yes, you have to have talent too. And you're right: There are some drummers who have made it despite not being technically or rhythmically the best or whatever. But they stayed on their path and made it happen, so hats off to them.

Some people get lucky and it happens quickly, but that's not really the general story out there. You don't get a knock on the door one day and find a tour bus parked outside with Radiohead saying, "Hey, we need a drummer. Want to join the band? Oh, and here's the keys to the kingdom." It's rare, far and few between. But we live in a world now where kids sit in their basements making rad YouTube videos of them playing other people's songs. And yes, they're getting gigs: they've never played a fucking show in their life (or left the basement or toured), and they're landing spots in the biggest bands in the world. We live in that world now. These are the new auditions happening. Most of these kids that are now in these big bands that you've never heard of before have a million YouTube subscribers—and they play Sum 41 and My Chemical Romance songs in their basements. That's a different world that we live in. But you know what? Fucking more power to them! They're talented and hustling in the virtual world we live in now, getting gigs and doing it.

But it's like, whatever you want to do in life, just fucking do it and don't stop until it happens. That really is the formula for achieving things. And if it hasn't happened yet, I feel like you strayed off your path somehow. There's no reason we can't accomplish anything we say we're gonna do if we just keep laser-focused tunnel vision. This is our path, this is our goal. We're not fucking stopping until it happens. That's my world, that's what I live in, that's what I live by, and that's all I know. Maybe it's just a me thing; I don't know…

Street Drum Corps always had special guests, and I've always done stuff with other artists, like the "drum moment" at The Alternative Press Music Awards with Adrian Young and Josh Dun of twenty one pilots. That's been something natural for me. I've never had a problem asking amazing musicians and drummers to be involved in Street Drum Corps shows or the projects that Tommy Lee and I have done. Everyone's always really come out and supported it. Even during the pandemic, Adrian came and surprised the kids at the School of Rock in Orange County. I asked him to come by, and he got up and played a Ramones song!

I've always had that relationship with artists, and obviously the drummers are usually down—we have this brotherhood thing. I wish others would use the spotlight they have on them for this kind of outreach. Can you imagine if one of these giant musicians was like, "I'm gonna to go do a fucking workshop with School of Rock and talk about suicide prevention and mental health and all this stuff"? I hope someone will and I hope I can inspire people to do that. It's not just about playing: Anyone can jam with kids. It's about knowing how to communicate, what to discuss, and being natural. I don't know how I have that gift.

And that's another thing: It takes a certain personality to perform and connect with these kids. That's the most special part about the workshops—it's the *conversation*. So hey, if I'm the guy, then I have no problem doing that; I'll just hunker down and make it happen. But School of Rock was saying they really want to turn this into an initiative, where they've got a guitar player, a bass player, a singer… I want to help make it happen, and I'm curious to see where it goes. Hopefully, all this light being shined on it will inspire some people to get off their asses and go make a difference. It's easy to write a fucking check for a charity. But it's about getting out there, connecting with the community, and giving these kids that face time.

Early on, I dreaded going for drum lessons because it was just fucking rudiments and reading. I just wanted to learn a Mötley Crüe song—I understood I had to learn that other stuff—but at my drum school, they weren't doing that. Then later on, I found a teacher who was cool. We did all the reading in the beginning, but then we had fun and rocked the fuck out at the end. He had a drum kit, and I had a drum kit, and we played whatever songs I wanted to learn. He taught me how to play the songs I liked. We'd get the business shit done, but then we'd have fun at the end.

And School of Rock is all about that. You learn your instrument, but then you get to be in a band and play gigs around town. You're a fucking rock star, you know? It's turned into such a fun place to learn. Learning is fun again, you know, with School of Rock, and there are a million other places out there for these kids to learn their craft. I'm sure it's the same way with any other trade, you know, with art schools and whatever. It's just a great time for learning, and it's come such a long way.

And learning *should* be fun. I'm watching the way my kids are learning math and reading, and it's in such a fun way. It's nothing like the way I learned, where it wasn't fun: you're stuck at a tiny desk for this many hours, facing the fucking blackboard, and the teacher droning on, the bell ringing, and all this stuff that was just miserable for me. It didn't work for me personally, but now I love seeing that learning can actually be fun. My kids are having a blast. I see them wake up in the morning, grab their books, and they're ready to learn.

My life has been a big balancing and juggling act. I do it to myself because I want to. Doing all this stuff completes me; I have so much passion and so many different things I want to do. Yes, it gets a little fucking wild sometimes, and I've got to pump the brakes or take some time off or whatever. But at least understanding that I need to acknowledge that so I don't create any mental health issues by spinning the fuck out instead of learning how to balance it on a healthy level.

Really, I need to decompress, sit on the couch with my wife and kids, and take it all in. My mom was coming out to California for the first time in years, and I just need to have that time just to get off the roller coaster for a minute and let it all sit in. But I'm sitting here, feeling really fucking proud of all the accomplishments this year, making the goals, hitting the marks, and letting them just resonate. It's fueling me to keep this going and fight for what I believe in for my career, my family, my communities… just *everything…*

It takes a lot out of me to hold all that shit together, for sure. But I love it. There's no autopilot—I've got it. I feel like I'm that air traffic controller just navigating the whole thing.

HellFest France 2025 with Electric Callboy
Photo credit: Dajoe Berlei

Backstage with Adrian Young & Josh Dun at the Alternative Press Awards (Cleveland, OH 2017)

Backstage warmup with coach Glenn Holmes at When We Were Young Festival (Las Vegas, 2023)

First show with Electric Callboy at Good Things Festival (Melbourne, Australia 2024)

Last time seeing Chester Bennington (Amsterdam, 2017)

Street Drum Corps in Bahrain on military tour (Middle East, 2014)

Bezerk performance with Tommy Lee & USC Drumline at Guitar Center Drum-Off (Los Angeles, 2010)

Congratulations!!!!

T B 4/26/2014

To Zummo

Apr 26, 2014 at 6:31 PM

Hey buddy, I'm sorry I couldn't make it last night! I hope you and your lovely bride had the night of your lives :) I'm very happy for you both and wish you nothing but the best in your lives together!

Chester

Email from Chester Bennington the day after my wedding (2014)

Crüefest 2 finale (East Coast, USA 2009)

Street Drum Corps with Chris Cornell backstage on Projekt Revolution (2008)

Sum 41 final show (Toronto, Canada 2025)

Email to Deryck Whibley that started my Sum 41 journey (2013)

-----Original Message-----
From: Deryck Whibley
To: Frank Zummo
Sent: Mon, Apr 22, 2013 3:09 pm
Subject: Re: Zummo

i live in LA. cool vids. but already know you're a bad ass drummer. i've seen you play a few times. i'd love to jam sometime. i just got off a really long tour. 3 years! way too long. i can't do that again. i'm pretty fucking burnt out. so anyway i'm taking a bit of a break from music right now. but lets stay in touch. maybe we can meet up in a bit even just for some drinks or something.

take care man. talk soon.

deryck

On Apr 22, 2013, at 2:38 PM, Frank Zummo wrote:

> Dope! Great to hear from ya brutha! All's been amazing bro!
> U livin in LA or Canada? Let's get up soon bro, it's been far too long!
> I also heard that Steve O left the band.
> I'd love to rock with you guys & would luv to discuss.
> Here's some of my drum vid's to peep:
> http://youtu.be/Xy8OSnRvrt0

Chester Bennington Celebration show finale at the Hollywood Bowl (Los Angeles, 2017)

My sister & I with our father, Frank Zummo Sr. (1980s)

Soundcheck at Sum 41's final show with my family in Toronto, Canada (2025)

Half Hollow Hills East high school marching band (New York, 1990s)

First recording session with Sum 41 (Hollywood, 2015)

Baby Zummo on my father's 1976 Ludwig drumkit (1980)

Good Morning America with Sum 41 (New York City, 2024)

The Great Wall of China with SJC's Mike Ciprari (2018)

My firstborn son, Brixton (2016)

Sum 41's induction into the Canadian Music Hall of Fame at the Juno Awards (Vancouver, 2025)

School of Rock Workshop (Phoenix, Arizona 2025)

Email from Tommy Lee after the Mötley Tour (2009)

tommylee
To Frank
Aug 30, 2009 at 11:00 AM
8/30/2009

1 attachment

Frank!....thank you again man!...And thanks for lookin after my son here and back!...means the world to me!!.....i owe ya!! Love and safe travels bro!!!!!!!

Tommy Lee
トミー リー
Be yourself. Everyone else is already taken.

Sum 41's final show, alongside my sons Riot & Brixton (Toronto, Canada 2025)

Nike Marathon with twenty one pilots' Josh Dun (Los Angeles, 2018)

Backstage at Street Drum Corps' Las Vegas residency with Stephen Perkins, Adrian Young & Tommy Lee (2013)

High school era in my parents' basement (New York, 1990s)

My sister & I with our Mother (Early 1980s)

My Nonny & I (New York, 1978)

Krewella live in Tokyo, Japan (2015)

In Kauai with Gabby Reece & Laird Hamilton (Hawaii, 2020)

With Shepard Fairey at Obey Studios (Los Angeles, 2018)

Email from Nikki Sixx after the Mötley Tour (2009)

Subject: Re: Zummo

it was a pleasure to have you out.you have made me a fan for life......anything i or the band can ever do for you..just call......thank you again frank..

Nikki

My second-born son, Riot (2018)

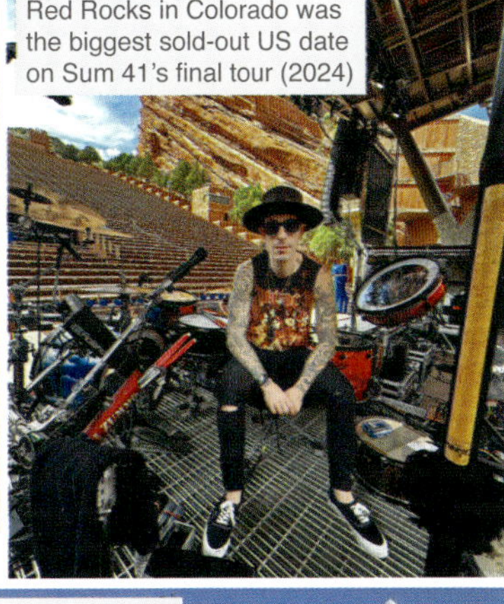
Red Rocks in Colorado was the biggest sold-out US date on Sum 41's final tour (2024)

Street Drum Corps at Vans Warped Tour with Bert McCracken (San Francisco, 2005)

In Jerusalem with Gary Numan (2014)

Reading & Leeds Festival with Mike Shinoda (UK, 2018)

Re: Goodnight!

Gary Numan 2/24/2014
To Frank Zummo
Feb 24, 2014 at 1:01 PM

Hey Frank,

Have a good, restful night and a safe flight tomorrow.

Thanks for the tour, you were fantastic. Great drumming, great bandmate, great company.

See you soon,

Gary.

Post-tour email from Gary Numan (2014)

The first night in Toronto on the final Sum 41 tour (2025)

The Zoo, my East Coast cover band out of high school (1996)

First show with Sum 41 at the Alternative Press Music Awards with DMC (Cleveland, OH 2015)

Drumming at the bottom of Laird Hamilton's pool for my "E.O.T.E." music video (Malibu, CA 2020)

Backstage at Chain Reaction with Aimee Echo & Adrian Young. First show with theStart: Adrian was my sub! (Anaheim, CA 2004)

Vans performance with Steve Van Doren & Mike Ciprari (2018)

The Drumheads have landed on Earth! (parts unknown, 2022)

Our wedding day with Reverend Dhani Harrison (Newport Beach, CA 2014)

Riding Tommy Lee's 360 Coaster with Lauren (Las Vegas, NV 2011)

With Anthony Bourdain (Boston, 2017)

Wedding Day with Poppa Frederic DeFeis (2014)

Elementary school Frank, jamming in my parents' basement (Brentwood, NY in the early 1980s)

Vans TV appearance with Kevin Lyman, Steve Caballero & Steve Van Doren (2021)

Coachella festival with Kayzo & special guests grandson, Yungblud, Alex Gaskarth & Tommy Lee (Indio, CA 2019)

Mini Street Drum Corps Zummo (NY, 1978)

Sum 41's set at Vans Warped Tour was Brixton's first concert (East Coast, 2016)

With Scott Weiland in Reno, Nevada (2013)

The Zummo family in Venezia, Italia (2024)

Maternity Photo 2015
Photo credit: Lisa Johnson

9
PRESENT AND ACCOUNTING

When I'm on tour, I take a moment onstage every night. Sometime during the show, it just hits me. I take it all in and look out into the nosebleed seats, remembering when I was up there at every single show. I take a moment to reflect, be present, and snap out of the chaos.

You can live in "a tour bubble." I don't have a problem with that. I don't see many solo shows in the near future—very few, actually—because of this demanding final tour. I want to be present and enjoy that schedule. I've battled with the question of whether I should be relaxing on a day off or driving however many hours to do a solo show. I'm not going to hustle like that because this is the final time; I want to enjoy it. I don't want to be exhausted.

We're headlining now. Last year, we were headlining, but we were playing 45 minutes to an hour max—which was nothing. Now that we're headlining on the final tour and playing this demanding new music, I'm not fucking around. I just want to enjoy it. I don't want to look back and think, *Fuck, man. I don't know what just happened. I didn't enjoy that. I was all over the place and I wasn't in it.* I'm making a very conscious effort in trying to be present in all aspects of everything I do. And I think this tour was a really good test of that.

Obviously, being in Mötley Crüe and being on tour with Tommy Lee is a book of its own. This is the great rock star story that, when I share it, people's jaws just drop on the floor. I'm in Mötley Crüe drumming for Tommy, but he's still on the tour, biding his time until he's able to play again.

He says to me backstage, "Hey, we have the next two days off, and the tour booked us at the Ritz-Carlton or Four Seasons or something on the water in West Palm Beach."

Sick. That'll be so fun.

"*Naaah*, we ain't doing *that*," he tells me. "When you get offstage, don't go to the dressing room, go directly to the bus. The assistant will grab all your shit, and we're going to have a police escort out of the venue."

A police escort? I've never had that in my life.

OK, the show's over. We get on the bus, the police escort is there, and we all head onto the highway. I ask Tommy where the fuck we're going. He says we're jumping on a private jet he chartered, and we're gonna go to the Bahamas and visit the Atlantis Resort for two days.

I have never been on a private jet in my life.

So we're off, hopping on this private jet. Mere hours after I get offstage, we're literally by the fucking ocean. For two days. Tommy and I leave our little cabana and head to the bar to order a drink, and Jay-Z is sitting there by himself, playing blackjack. He was there with Beyoncé, but Jay's alone, casually playing blackjack in board shorts and no shirt, drinking a Corona.

Tommy had met him once before, so he says, "What's up," and Jay's like, "Come join me." So it's me, Tommy, and Jay-Z in shorts and no shirts, playing blackjack. I don't know how to play blackjack so Jay taught me. I had a $50 bill on me, so I put it in and I turned that $50 into $500. I won $500 and I have barely gambled since... Because why the fuck would I? That story is the best luck story ever, and I'm not even into gambling.

Then the next day, we woke up in the morning and we swam with dolphins. Again, the first time I ever did *that.*

We got on the jet and landed in West Palm. There was a tour bus waiting that took me right to the venue. An hour later, I was onstage playing with Mötley. I had a microphone that would go directly into Tommy's in-ear monitors offstage. I said, "Dude! We were just swimming with dolphins. And now I'm playing for you to 30,000 people in West Palm Beach! Like, what the fuck?!" and I start laughing.

Mötley was paying me to play these shows, which was great: I would have paid *them* to play the dates. I remember looking at my account and they had made a deposit. I had just turned 31. I was still on Interscope as well, where Street Drum Corps had the big, Jimmy Iovine record deal. I remember looking at my bank account and I was like, "Oh, my God, I'm rich." Obviously, I wasn't, but it was the most money I ever had in my bank account. I remember just being like, *Holy shit, I fucking made it...*

And then fast-forward to a year later or whenever it was we got dropped. Suddenly, I had no more money because we were on salary then—and now it's gone. But that's the ups and downs of my career. I would say that I was at my lowest when I moved to LA and I spent all the money I had saved to live there on my car that blew up on the way down. My band didn't fucking happen like it was supposed to, and I had to get a job. I'm on my own here: I've got to pay for my apartment, all my bills, *everything...*

Now I sit in my studio and look at all these incredible memories I'm surrounded by. I have never *ever* sold drums. When I was a kid, I would trade in drums I wasn't using to get others I wanted. I never sold them to pay rent—that was never a fucking option. I'd willingly subsist on pints of water if it meant having to sell my gear. I've still got my dad's Ludwigs that I learned on, sitting in my studio to this day. My boys know how important those are. I've got my Shepard Fairey hand-painted and printed, one-of-a-kind drum set. Those are my two most prized possessions. And then the first drums that I ever bought when I graduated high school in 1996. I just shipped them to my home here in California. My boys refurbished them with me, and now they're in their playroom—that's really special.

I did some reflecting last night while driving my mom to the airport. This holiday season felt even more special for me, one of the best. I think the reason is that I was present. I finally had a chance to get off the rollercoaster; it felt like everything stopped for me. The first week of December, everything stopped. The previous year, I was in Australia until, I don't know, December 20th or something like that. I came home, it was Christmas, and then right after the holiday, I had to debut the Drumheads show and rehearse that. So I wasn't really present because I came through the other side of a whirlwind year of touring, prior to introducing the Drumheads.

This year, it was done. I had the whole month to get off the rollercoaster and just fucking smell the roses and just truly be present. And for me to be present and switch off, it takes me a minute; it takes me a while to wind down and really think about things. My mom was here for the first time in five years, and the kids are at this age where they're growing so fast and they're still so in love with the holidays. I took the time to just step back, take snapshots, and just really disconnect and not think about work. We took the kids to their Christmas present, an indoor waterpark resort for the night. And Lauren was like, "I haven't seen you smile this much in so long." If my family noticed it enough to comment, it just proves that being present is so important.

I remember when SDC were on tour with Thirty Seconds to Mars. That band just blew up. I remember how massive "The Kill" was back then. They were on every talk show, and I was on their bus with them. (SDC would all split up, and we'd be on different buses on that tour. I rode with those guys.)

I remember one night sitting in the front lounge alone with Jared Leto. And he was like, "Dude, I don't even know what's going on. We're here, we're there. I'm editing a video; I can't even enjoy it." I remember that resonating with me like, *this guy's got everything you'd ever dream of. Right now, it's happening… and he's not even enjoying it.* Not to say he *wasn't* enjoying it, but it was hard to be present. He was in so deep by that point.

This year, this holiday, was just one of the best for me ever because I was *just present*. I think it's a theme in life to just somehow get off that roller coaster, have some time to decompress because it makes life so much more enjoyable and meaningful and special.

If you had told me to pick 10 friends that I was concerned about, Chester Bennington wouldn't have been on that list, at all. Especially since I had seen him that summer, right before he passed away. We played two shows together. He was lovely and stoked and happy. I knew he had addiction problems where he was off and on with substance abuse. I didn't know about the suicidal dark side. That was beyond shocking.

Chester lived with Ryan Shuck at times. Chester's wife was Ryan's friend—he introduced them. I think Ryan was battling similar things and that's why they were dear friends: They connected on that level. But that stuff wasn't really shared with me. I think he and Ryan shared those things more, and Ryan knew the darkness Chester had inside of him. I wasn't on that level of understanding and knowing.

So honestly, at that point, I didn't know how to deal with it. I really hadn't dealt with that stuff in the groups I was in full time. Thankfully, I was in a band with healthy people, like Street Drum Corps. I learned how to deal when drinking got the best of Deryck and he ended up in the hospital. But he wasn't suicidal. I didn't know the resources or how to address certain situations because mental health and substance abuse didn't really come up. I didn't come from a home where we had any of those issues, thankfully.

We talk about "rock star stories," and this one is near the top of the list; it's pretty rad. I've always loved Anthony Bourdain's show, *Parts Unknown*. I really loved his takes on dining and food, his insights about it, and the traveling aspect of the show. Whenever I'm in a city, it's like, what's the place to go to? What's the food from that culture? His show was one of my favorites just because I'm a traveler and I love great food and all that. I fell in love with his show and him as a person. And he's such a music person—he's had all these people from Iggy Pop to ?uestlove on his shows.

He put out a cookbook and my wife got it for me. He was doing a book tour that sold out and we couldn't go. He was talking at the Pantages Theater in Hollywood, and it sold out. I was bummed. But Lauren's like, "You know what? You're going to cross paths when the time is right."

Fast-forward to like a year or two later, and SJC Drums gets invited to do this TV show called *Raw Craft*, where they find incredible craft makers from all over the world who make amazing stuff and share their stories. There's one episode about an Italian suit maker, one about drums, and the show is sponsored by Balvenie, a very high-end whiskey brand. This particular episode was about making a snare drum from a Balvenie whiskey barrel.

So they made this snare drum for Tre Cool from Green Day and delivered the drum to him at his show. Anthony Bourdain was the host. Mike from SJC Drums is a dear, dear friend of mine. He said, “Hey, we’re doing a screening of the show in Boston over Thanksgiving weekend. You’re going to be visiting your family. Why don’t you come up, attend the screening of our episode? There’s going to be a whiskey tasting, like a very bougie event. And, you know, you get to meet Anthony.”

I went up and they played the episode and Anthony and Mike talked about everything. I thought I’d maybe meet him real quick—you know, just a casual, “Hey, nice to meet you,” shake hands. Turns out Mike brings me into Anthony’s dressing room, and after everything is done, it’s just Anthony and me. We talked for fucking hours. Music! Life! Food! Like one of the most amazing conversations I’ve ever had. And it was just such a special, special night. I have a great picture of us together from that night. And it was just like, “Wow, Lauren was right.” This was far better than just sitting in the audience of his show. I got to have this experience and have this amazing night with somebody that I really look up to. It was incredible.

A couple of months later, I wake up and Lauren’s like, “Hey, I’ve got bad news. I just saw Anthony took his life.” And I was just like, “What the fuck?” It was a heavy time. Going from [Chris] Cornell to Chester, Scott Weiland to Anthony… There are a lot of people I really idolized. And, you know, they shouldn’t have been gone. It was just a big wake-up call for me to do whatever I had to do to not be in a similar situation. And then out of that darkness, it inspired me on a personal level to keep my shit together and stay on that path. And then figure out: What can I do for everyone else with the spotlight I have on me? What can I raise its light on? What can we do and how can we do it?

My life mantra is that everything is a teachable moment. Whenever something negative happens, I ask myself, *how do I change it so I don’t feel that way*? There are just so many things that rub me the wrong way. Being a New Yorker, I see how fucking high-strung people are, how they fly off the fucking handle at the drop of a hat. I was like, *I can’t ever become that.* It would just make me feel so horrible, that feeling of like, *really*? Like disrespecting somebody, at a fucking subway station because they don’t know how to use the ticket machine. It’s like, *Are you fucking kidding me?* It would be like a mental reminder here. *Don’t become this. Learn from this change.*

I had a shuttle driver here in the country. He used to work for Apple, but he retired. He always took me to the airport. Every tour I went on, he picked me up, and he'd pick me up when I'd come back. Just a great older gentleman, always there for me. I find out he was driving one of his clients to the airport last week and a fucking pickup truck came into his lane on this two-lane road and hit him head-on, killing him and his passenger. His life is over, but his whole family just lost their dad, grandfather, *everything*, right before Christmas. I had spent so much time with this guy. It was a wake-up call, reminding me that I can't take anything for granted. So while we're here, let's just enjoy it.

My mom's 70 now. That's why I made sure to really take the time to just *make* that special time, even if it's the last night. Instead of just dropping her off at the airport, I parked, I walked her in, I checked her bag, and I walked her through all the way to the TSA. It was like a movie. I hugged her goodbye, and she walked toward the TSA line.

Instead of just turning around and leaving, I sat there. I watched her walk away. It only took a moment: We live far apart. I don't get to see her often. I just want to be present and have this memory.

Life could be short.

RESOURCES:

988 Lifeline: 988lifeline.org Text or Chat to: 988

Society for the Prevention of Teen Suicide: sptsusa.com

To Write Love on Her Arms: twloha.com

Give an Hour: giveanhour.org

10
LA FAMIGLIA

If you're starting out in a band and you're going on your first tour, the one piece of advice I'll give you is this: Don't waste your money on rent. It's not a place that you own. How much stuff do you really have? You're not there. Is it wise to waste that cash when you're making a minimal income?

I kinda took that to heart, and theStart were very generous, letting me put my stuff in their band storage area and crash at their place. Once Street Drum Corps started happening, Bobby and Adam both found themselves in a similar situation, either breaking up with girlfriends they were living with or dealing with roommate issues or whatever. But their mom had a solution. "Listen, I have this big house in Redondo Beach. Why don't you guys just come stay here and get this Street Drum Corps thing going?"

It was pretty amazing. We each had a room rent-free, and we built that business on the floor. We would sit in Bobby's bedroom on the floor with our computers and strategize, "How are we going to go on the Warped Tour? What companies are we reaching out to?" We built the business and then we started touring, and she was like, "Leave your stuff here. You guys have minimal breaks. Just stay here." It was really nice because I'm a big family person, and I didn't have family there; they quickly became my family.

When Street Drum Corps got our Interscope deal, we had a business manager. I remember being on the Linkin Park tour and calling him to ask, "Can I afford my own place? I don't want to live with someone else. I want to get my own place and be an adult. Buy my own furniture." He replied, "Yeah, absolutely." It was back in the Craigslist days, and I found an amazing apartment in the same Valley Village neighborhood where we once rented a home studio to record SDC demos.

I found this amazing place with a wonderful landlady. I lived there for a long time, and I just remember it was the coolest feeling to come home from that tour, driving up and thinking, *This is my own place.* I could go shopping, buy my own stuff, and not have to live in other people's homes anymore. It was a really great feeling.

I was out in Hollywood one night—not really wanting to go out—but I was entertaining some people that were in town from Europe. They wanted to hit up a club in Hollywood and do that whole scene, which I didn't do. But I went, and the people I was with were just out of control—drunk, just getting sloppy. People were wanting to fight them; it was embarrassing. So I literally escaped to the stage. I only went there because my drum tech at the time had previously worked with the DJ. They were onstage, and I just went up there because I needed a break from the chaos.

I went up onstage, and there was this beautiful girl standing there. I just went up to her and started talking. Her name was Lauren, and she was there because the percussion player's tech had invited her. I discovered that we both shared that feeling of not really wanting to be there.

As we talked, we realized that our bands had played shows together. When I was in theStart, we were on the same record label—not Nitro, but later on when theStart moved to Metropolis. Her band was A Kiss Could Be Deadly, and we had shared stages in Riverside together where she was attending school. Back when Street Drum Corps was having dinner at The Slidebar in Orange County with Adrian Young, her band was performing there. I didn't meet her then, but I did meet her band members. Bobby and Adam hung out in her tour van with her and her band members, *but* not me!

We figured out, "Whoa, we've been to all these places together." We had literally played shows together—you know, passing ships over the years. Well, her band started getting into songwriting for other people, and I guess she and Bobby from SDC had such a great chat that her band wrote and submitted a song for the Street Drum Corps record back then, and I didn't even know. We were getting submissions all the time, but I didn't know her then.

She was living in Orange County at the time. And then fast-forward: I had a show in Orange County with DJ Aero. I'd been doing a drumming/DJ thing with him for a while. She came out… and that was it. She was living between Orange County and Northern California, where her family was. I wound up flying up to Northern California to go on holiday to visit her because she was up there.

I actually met her dad, and she told me about her family. Because that's the thing for me—family is so important. You can be the raddest girl in the world, but if there's a lot of family trouble or parents aren't in the picture or whatever, it's a turnoff. Because I just love family. I appreciate the solid foundations families provide because that's what I come from, what I know, and I'm comfortable with it. I got burned being with a lot of girls who just didn't have good, healthy family relationships, or I wouldn't meet their parents because they weren't in the picture. It just never sat well with me for some reason.

In the summer of 2010, Lauren ended up moving in with me because she was touring. I was like, "You can stay here because I want to see you." She stayed with me, and her parents came down to visit; we went to dinner, the whole thing. (Funnily enough, Lauren was in town visiting me on tour recently, and we went back to that place: It's called Firefly, and it's still there in Studio City.) I just fell in love with her parents. They stayed at the house with us, and we spent the whole weekend with them. It was really cool that they drove down there to meet their daughter's new boyfriend. Lauren was the first woman I had ever been with who made me totally feel like I could tell her *everything*.

I was coming out of my Mötley Crüe, single-guy phase from all the success that had finally happened. I was out in the world, getting all this attention, being in these amazing situations and enjoying my life as a bachelor. When I met Lauren, I was one foot in and one foot out of that world; it was still exciting, but I wanted to settle down. And it finally got to a point where she reached ultimatum time. She asked me point-blank, "Are you serious about this? Are you ready to commit? Otherwise, I'm out of here." I didn't know she had been secretly collecting boxes to move out because she didn't think things were going to work out. It was a rocky time. I just owned up. I told her, "I am 100 percent in, and I don't want to lose you. Let's do this." We got totally serious, and it was really cool to be with someone I could share *everything* with, and honestly tell her stuff that I had never told anyone.

I asked for her dad's permission. He has three daughters, including Lauren. He teared up and said none of their spouses had asked his permission. So that was meaningful for him, especially since she's his youngest daughter. We went to Napa, and I proposed to her at dinner with my Nonny's wedding ring. It was amazing and nerve-wracking at the same time.

We made our wedding something really cool instead of that whole, stressful dinner thing where nobody even eats. We just said, "Let's make it a party. Let's make it a destination," because people were coming in from New York, Florida, and Northern California. We wanted to create a destination wedding for them, so we wound up getting married on a boat in Orange County. It sailed around the harbor, and when it came time to choose who would marry us, a staffer on the boat said, "Hey, we have a captain who can marry you."

Now as cool as that sounded to me, being at the altar, saying our vows, and getting married is something that I wanted to feel totally comfortable with. This is a "royal" thing. Who do I know that feels like the most regal person for this? I was in Dhani Harrison's band, thenewno2. We were very close, and he's such an amazing human. He accepted my request and took it seriously. He got certified, embraced it, and it was really beautiful.

We turned it into a three-day event. We had a wedding rehearsal dinner at the test kitchen owned by Ryan Shuck from Julien-K, Dead by Sunrise, and Orgy. He was creating this beautiful gourmet pizza place that wasn't even open yet. We planned this whole amazing experience just for our wedding party and immediate family. That was night one. Night two was the wedding on the boat. And night three, we ended up having a taco truck backyard event. We stretched it into a three-day celebration since everyone was traveling from far away. Then we went to Hawaii for our honeymoon.

We'd been together long enough, and we're married now, so let's start trying to have a kid... We had our first son, Brixton, in early 2016, which was insane. Days before, the doctor had told us his due date was around New Year's Eve. And Krewella had a big gig in Washington, D.C., on New Year's Eve.

Krewella were like, "Are you able to do it? We want to accommodate you because we know your wife could go into labor at any moment. We're down to literally have flights ready if you need to leave ASAP." My drum tech was trained to know the show in case he had to sub for me. They flew me in at the last minute. I literally went there, played the show, and went back to the airport—I didn't even stay at the hotel—flew home, had Wi-Fi on the plane, and checked in with Lauren. They were incredibly accommodating, and it was fun to play a show with them on New Year's.

There's a tradeshow convention in Anaheim for the fairs that Street Drum Corps is part of. I go every year, and Justin from the Drumheads would often come with me. Lauren's still all good. She's like, "Go to the convention. You can drive home from Anaheim if need be." My mom also was in town. So we finished the first day of the trade show, and I went up to the hotel to just chill for a minute. But then Lauren calls, and she's like, "It's go-time. You need to come home." I was like, "Shit, It's rush hour and I'm in Anaheim. Just get ready, I'll keep you posted."

In some miraculous way, someone was looking out for me: there was no traffic! I made it home, got her and my mom in the car, and went to the hospital. And like typical newbie parents, we got there too early. We were almost going to have to leave and go home, but then she showed signs of being ready to have the baby. So he was born the next morning.

You know, it was a crazy experience being in the hospital. There were so many people in and out. I was trying to be supportive, but I was also there to witness my son being born. It was a wild first day. The coolest part was that her parents made it in time to be in the room, and my mom was there. So we had all of our parents present.

After Brixton was maybe one or two years old, we finally bought our first house. Lauren, the dog, and I had outgrown my townhouse-style apartment. The neighborhood started going downhill, but by that point, I had some money; I had been saving the entire time I was in Sum 41. We bought a house in Woodland Hills and it was amazing. Everything was like a small, perfect *home*. It had beautiful views; it was like a dream living up in the canyon, taking in those epic views. It was our first home where we could really decorate and make family memories.

Not long afterward, Lauren got pregnant with our second son, Riot. We decided, since we weren't that thrilled with the hospital experience, that Lauren wanted to prepare for a home birth. You have to be prepared for this, because it is all about the baby's health and safety. She hired an incredible doula. We were set up to either have the baby at home or have a bag packed to take to the hospital.

We put Brixton to bed one night, and Lauren started having contractions. I called her doula; she said she was on her way. She arrived, checked Lauren's vitals, and she's like, "This baby's coming. We don't have time to go to the hospital. It's go-time." So I had to jump in and help her. It was me, the doula, and my mother-in-law. I was there to support my wife with whatever made her comfortable. She's the one doing all this work and everything. It was the most amazing, beautiful experience ever. I fully got to help receive the baby, cut the cord, and just enjoy the experience because we weren't in the hospital with a million people coming in and out, feeling stressed in that environment.

It was probably four in the morning when we finally went to bed—in our own house—and it was great. Our dog was even in the room with us. It was just so chill. As we're about to go to bed, Lauren goes, "Well, I guess you can go to that studio session tomorrow. The baby is healthy. My mom's here. Go to your session."

I had a session booked that I completely forgot about because we went into baby-mode and I forgot to cancel it. I was going into EastWest Studios to record my first solo single, "The Less We Know," with Kayzo, as well as his lead single "Cruel Love." I slept for a few hours, then I packed up my drums in the car, went to the studio, and was on the highest of highs after all that had happened. It was the most magical and special session ever.

Parenting is the greatest and hardest thing. You know, I used to think touring and traveling and the flights and the airports and not sleeping was hard. Now when I go on tour, it feels like a vacation. Because at home with two young kids and a house, it's nonstop. When they were babies, that was a lot of hard work, just learning. Then when you go from one to two children, it's a whole other thing—but it's the most *amazing* thing.

But I'm also worrying for the rest of my life. I will worry about them, their well-being and everything. I've helped create these humans, which is just the most incredible thing. I don't care how many movies or videos you've watched: Until you're there and you've experienced it, it's genuinely a miracle and incredible in every way.

I have a deep respect for women, stemming from being raised by my mom. When my dad left after my parents split, I became the man of the house, for real. My sister is three years younger, and I was really helping to take care of the family. But actually seeing the birth process and what women go through up until the point they have the baby is truly incredible.

Lauren stopped touring: She and her songwriting partner became a team and they were getting placements in TV shows and whatnot. She wound up getting a job with her uncle doing health care recruitment, and she kicked ass. She enjoyed it, but it got harder once we had kids because it's a job for people without families—it's a grind. Once we started a family, I think it was hard for her to balance it.

Then the pandemic hit, all my touring got taken away. I was supposed to go to Mexico for a Sum tour and was at the airport, but was told to go home. That was it. But Lauren, she still had a steady job. She supported the family during that time, which was amazing. We live in California: both partners have to work (unless you're a billionaire). But Lauren carried us through. She made a major pivot and now she runs the community learning center our kids attend.

In between the final Sum show in Toronto and the Junos, I looked at Lauren and said, "We didn't celebrate our 10-year anniversary last year because I was on tour, but I have a little break now. I've been gone for so long. When I'm home, we're caught up in family madness and sports and, you know, just *life*. You and I haven't gone away since our honeymoon—which is now 11 years ago—for more than two nights without the kids. I need to go reset after all this and just reflect and reconnect with you."

We did a last-minute trip to Kauai. I reached out to the amazing Laird Hamilton and Gabby Reece for some advice because my wife and I had our honeymoon in Kauai but we hadn't been back in a while. Since they live there part-time, they said, "We just left, but our house is yours. Go enjoy."

Lauren and I stayed there. It was paradise. We'd walk down their driveway, jump on paddle boards, my wife and I, and it was so magical in so many ways.

I went there to reset, but I came back more in love with my wife and more reconnected than ever. I'm really grateful that I had that realization, because I want my marriage to stay strong and to work on it at all times.

LAUREN ZUMMO, lead vocalist of A Kiss Could Be Deadly and Electric Valentine; co-founder and operations director for a NorCal learning center providing enrichment classes for homeschool families; loving wife and Mom:

Our paths crossed several times before we really even noticed each other—which is kind of funny. My first band was A Kiss Could Be Deadly, and he was drumming for theStart. I went to school out in Riverside, California. We played a local show with theStart at this bar and it was a big deal for us. The drummers would always set up their drum kits right outside because there was no backstage. Everyone hung out in their cars or vans or whatever in the parking lot or gathered in the back and went into the building at showtime. So you had to pass by the drummers every time to get into the club. I know I must have met him at some point and said hello.

There was another show where he came to see my next band, Electric Valentine. We played at the Slidebar in Fullerton. The place was big and there were several different rooms, so he never actually saw my band play because he was hanging out with people in other rooms. I did meet Bobby and Adam that night, and my band and I found out that they were working on a Street Drum Corps album. So we decided to write a song for them called "Beat Drop" and submitted it to them. They didn't do anything with it, so we ended up using it for ourselves. Our kids love that song now—it's one of their favorites, probably because of the story.

Once, when neither of us were in a relationship, we both happened to go to the same club in Hollywood one night to see a DJ/drum performance. He was friends with the DJ tech and I was friends with the drum tech. The friend I was with said, "That's Frank from Street Drum Corps." And I'm like, "What? I kind of know them. We wrote a song for them, but I never met *him*." At that point, that's when we caught each other's attention. All these times our paths crossed, we never actually met, but that's ultimately how it all happened.

After Street Drum Corps' Interscope deal wasn't renewed, I believe it was a pivotal moment for him, and he had to start focusing on what was next. That's what I think is pretty amazing about Frank: He'll shift where he needs to and get focused or refocus, get creative, think about how he can take something and approach it differently—and then he starts putting it out to the universe. Because he loves to perform. He loves to be onstage drumming. He could do all the studio stuff—and

I think that's all great—but ultimately his heart is on the stage, drumming and performing. I remember there was one day where... maybe it was like the Sunset Strip Music Festival or something like that... and he played with three bands in one day.

He's got a drive that inspires. If you're someone who can learn by observation, he's a great one to observe. But Frank's not soulless. He has that capacity to still be a human, even though he's so regimented. But I'm in a unique position as his wife, because down time is different, and he's going to be working a lot when he's home. I see that, but also, I can be the one to remind him, *put the phone down*, *be present.* You know, those kinds of things. But I feel like when he's outside of the home and making sure the machinery is moving as it needs to be, he's still able to appreciate the significance.

Frank is always churning and thinking and finding ways to do things. It's amazing. It's almost like an octopus. Have you ever seen an octopus when they put them in these obstacle courses? You see them and you're like, "There's no way this octopus is going to get to that shrimp" or whatever it is—and somehow it does. It finds a way, and you're like, "How did it squeeze through that little crevice?" You know, it's like where does he come up with this stuff? I think it's a really cool aspect that he brings so much to the table in whatever he does. Whatever he's passionate about and believes in, he'll take it as far as he can go.

Sometimes he'll start giving me updates on this situation or that situation, and I'm like, "OK, wait. What are you talking about right now? What are you referring to? Back up. Hold on." Sometimes, there are so many things going on. When one major thing ends, his wheels start turning and he starts grinding and hustling and doing his thing. Then things start coming in, and all of a sudden it's like, "Oh, my gosh! There's so much going on." Which is great. It's amazing, but I think it can become overwhelming at times because he actually is human. Believe it or not.

I will say that, in a real human way, at first, he'll sometimes feel disappointment—there are those human emotions that he will feel—if something doesn't work out like he wanted it to. He can definitely feel those emotions and be down about it or upset or experience a range of emotions. In time, though, he will somehow... I don't know what goes on in his brain... but he somehow takes it and refocuses and pivots. He's a master pivoter!

When we first started dating, I was still in a band. I was still doing shows and short, smaller tours. We weren't quite going as far as we did before, but we were still doing stuff. And it worked: he was doing his thing, I was doing my thing, and then we met in the middle. When my band started to fade out more, I then realized

I needed to have more going on here for myself, too. I needed to start making some money, so I ended up getting a part-time job.

As the relationship progressed, I thought, "I can be in a relationship with someone like this, right? That's fine. When he's doing his thing, I do my thing. Then we'll come back together, and that should be fine. I can work in a relationship like that. Not everybody can, though, you know? But I had no idea—and I don't think you can until you're in that position—of what it would be like when we had kids. I had no idea how him being on the road and coming and going would impact our future children. There's no amount of foresight that will prepare you for that—at least for me. Maybe other people have that foresight or had it. I started to see how this actually impacts our children when he leaves for a while. And then how do I, as the remaining parent, stay present in the moment? How do I manage that, how do I handle that? How do I help my kids navigate through that? And that has been really challenging in many ways. For them, especially.

Then there are times when he's working. He's on the road, in his routine, and very disciplined; he has a certain amount of time he has to warm up and certain things he does leading up to that. It's great that he's figured out what works for him, and how to keep his body going at maximum capacity.

There'll be times when the boys are having a hard time or I'm having a hard time with the boys. He'll be in the middle of everything in his world and his stuff's going on, and he's like, "Yeah, I'll be there, I'm in the middle of this or that," but it's like, "They need a dad *right now*. They need you to take a moment and be present—you're not here, but we do have FaceTime." I've definitely had to interrupt him. I'm sure there have been times when he's probably irritated that I'm not just handling the whole thing, right? I'm sorry, this is a dad thing right now, and because it's a *dad* thing, they need *you* right now. I understand you're busy with your thing and you're working and you're on tour, but you're gonna have to take a quick time-out here. So there are definitely times like that.

I know it's hard for anyone to stop their productivity, train of thought, and momentum, and then suddenly redirect. But that's just what happens when you have kids, right? I don't know. But, with all that being said, getting back to the inspiration part: I feel like we balance each other out because he's so focused on this mission and this path, and I'm on the other side where I'm taking in the beauty of the world. I'm letting that distract me, willingly, because I love that about the world. I think I've helped him at times to slow down and smell the roses, you know? And I hope I've inspired in him the urge to unplug and detach every once in a while. Be a human and turn the robot off for the day, you know?

There are many times when he'll dedicate performances to family members or people who have passed or to the boys or whomever. For some reason, there's something in that place, at that time, or in his hopes and dreams for the future of his family. Frank is not all robot. He will totally take the time and appreciate things; he's got a sentimental side that pops out. I think that's the same side that comes out when he's in these workshops and sees the impact that these very positive conversations can have.

I still sometimes have to remind him to unplug. We're having family time, and I can see him checking his emails or something coming in on his watch. It's like, "Hey, can we have family time?" And he's like, "Oh yeah." There still are those times when I have to remind him of that. But on the flipside of that, he brings structure where I don't always have it, you know? And I appreciate that. So maybe that's another piece of the puzzle for our kids. You know, when Dad leaves, a significant structure figure is leaving. And I provide structure, but in a much more loose, go-with-the-flow way. I'm sure in a few years, after they go to therapy, I'll hear about how that impacted them… [*Laughs.*]

11
DEAR FATHER

Really, I can't tell you about a friend, a rockstar, or anyone else I've had to cut off who has meant so much to me. There's only one person I had to cut out of my life because he refused to get help. And it's the fucking worst. It was my dad.

My dad was my role model who had his shit together until I hit high school. He definitely had baggage, but when we were young, we didn't notice. He was a great father—he really was. Baseball, music, drums, anything—he was *there*. He was an amazing father. Then, around high school, he and my mom just grew apart. They were getting divorced, and it got ugly. I was touring with my cover band on weekends, while my sister was home for a lot of the fights and all the shit that came with it. When my parents divorced, he reverted back to his old ways, went down a fucking spiral, and moved to Florida to try and start over but never did get back on his feet.

His brother, who is my godfather, literally said to him, "Don't turn into Dad." Don't turn into his father with my sister and me, because my dad had no relationship with them in the end. Once my parents got married, he cut his parents off. His parents were horrible, and they did a lot of awful, fucked-up shit. They weren't in my life: I had met them only a couple of times. My grandfather died, and I met my grandmother later in life. I met her again out of respect, and I would see her occasionally, but was very phony; I was just being respectful. My uncle warned him "not to be what he hated and have your kids cut you off." And he did become his fucking parents and died just like they did—not having their kids in their lives and all that kind of shit.

So yeah, my father wasn't at my wedding. He was invited, but he didn't show up. That's because I un-invited him. He got really nasty at a time when that wasn't what it was about. I invited him; he was coming. His health wasn't the best at that time. My dear friend John Sawicki said, "Hey, I got your dad. You've got a lot on your plate. I'll share a room with him. I'll help him out." Great! I had him all set.

So as I mentioned, Lauren and I got married on a boat. There was a capacity issue because it's a boat—there are rules and regulations. We split the cost of the wedding with my wife's parents. We were on a tight budget; it's like we *really had* to make it work. My mom paid for the rehearsal dinner, which was incredibly generous of her and something she had to save for for a long time. And you know, my family's not wealthy. My wife's family is not wealthy either; they worked hard for their money. But we made it *work*.

So my dad calls and asks if he could bring a date. And I'm like, "You have a girlfriend?" He replies, "No, I just want to bring a date. I don't want to go stag. I don't like going solo." Like *what*?

I explained it to him nicely. I said, "I don't think that's cool to ask for because my wife's family is paying for half of this wedding, and she has a giant family. We're over capacity. It's stressing people out because we can't invite second cousins and their significant others. And Mom's paying for the rehearsal dinner. You know, it's just not a good look for you. If you had a serious girlfriend or partner, that's a different story. But you don't even know who you're going to bring. It's not a good look, man." He took it badly and got offended.

I said, "And by the way, I got you covered. My buddy John's going to take care of you. You're not going to be alone. He's even gonna stay with you. We're all good. We got this worked out." Positive, right? He just flipped it and got really, really nasty. This is what the traditional Zummos do when there's a problem: They'll just start throwing other people under the bus who have nothing to do with the situation, which makes no sense.

When he started saying nasty stuff about my grandfather on my mother's side, Poppa DeFeis, who bailed my dad out of so many debts and issues, that was the end of it. My dad's own parents were not in his life because they were simply not good people. So I was just like, "Listen man, this is not cool. There's no reason to disrespect my grandfather. He has nothing to *do* with this, you know? This is my breaking point. I've done everything to try to help you. I bailed you out of so many financial messes, like paying for storage units for your stuff because you were living in your car and we didn't want your belongings to get taken away. Getting calls because you got arrested while living in your car—and they found stolen tags on your plates. You're never going to admit to my sister and I that you're a drug addict. I'm done. I've done everything I can do. I'm now the adult here, starting my own life, and I can't take care of you and deal with this, especially when you're going to disrespect me at the wedding and just create drama."

He found out through someone on social media that I had a kid, and he sent me a nasty voicemail. "You had a kid, and I didn't even know about it. That's just not cool." Now you would think he would have just been like, "Let's squash this.

I want to meet your kid. I want to be in his life. I'll come fly out," but it was just negative. So I didn't call him back. I'm not dealing with that. I'm just not engaging with toxic people I've tried everything with who aren't going to change.

And then I forgot what happened, but he was in the hospital and—same thing. Got a nasty message like, "You better call me because if this is the end, and if I don't make it, you're gonna regret this." Just more dicky inconsiderate stuff. And I'm like, *This guy, even on his deathbed, is being a dick.* I guess he had a stroke—I forget if he was driving—and then he was in a coma. My sister went to Florida: We knew he wasn't going to pull through. She went there, his brother (my godfather) lived in Florida as well.

I tried and tried and tried. My sister and I did whatever we had to do, but he just kept letting his health go, letting drugs overtake him, living in his fucking car, and just deny, deny, deny… And here's what I tell my children: *Just be honest. You will not get in trouble if you tell us the truth.* And my own dad wouldn't tell the truth about his fucking crack habit and all this shit.

I was about to leave for my first album cycle with Sum 41. We had a nine-week European tour, the longest, most consistent tour I had ever done in my life. I told the band my dad had passed away and I might have to go to Florida. I'll obviously still make this tour, but I may need to fly from Florida to the first show in Europe. They were like, "Yeah, whatever you need."

And Christie said, "Don't come. Dad's gone. You just had a kid and you're about to leave for nine weeks. Stay home with your family. You don't need to see him like this. I'm closer in New York to Florida. I can deal with this." She is a saint for doing that and let me have that time with my new baby.

Christie went to his trailer-park housing and found crack pipes and all the shit that I am so glad I didn't have to see. And it just reaffirmed everything. When she got to the hospital before he passed, she put the phone by his ear. I said my piece, and that was that.

CHRISTIE POIRIER: We both, unfortunately, hadn't been speaking to my dad for a year or two, and then his health completely declined. We had a complicated relationship with him from our teenage years onward. There were a lot of ups and downs; that's just how he was.

Our dad was a good guy, he was a sweetheart, he just… He had his own personal issues that unfortunately got in the way of our relationship with him. We had to let go and just be adults. And that was really hard. But we always made these decisions together. It wasn't like, "Well, you do what you want to do. I'm going to do what I want to."

Frank and I would have long conversations about it because we needed to be on the same page—after all, we're a unit. When my parents got divorced, I think my dad left when I was like 15, so Frank was 18, he took on the role of Dad a bit for me. So I wanted to give him back that stability, because he had a brand new son. Brixton was a baby, and Frank was about to go on tour for three months and wouldn't see them. So when I was in Florida, talking with him about Dad, and he's like, "I'll come, of course. You don't have to deal with this whole thing," I just told him, "He's gone, it's not gonna change if you're here or not. He's not here anymore."

My dad's brother, Uncle Charlie, we were very close with, and he was with me. And we had family friends who were also there for us. I felt like I had a good support team around me and I'm also a strong person, myself. But Frank was on the phone with me like every hour with every decision that had to be made, so he still was with me the whole time. He wasn't like, "Alright, cool. You got this, thanks." It was like all the little decisions that you have to make when someone passes, what that looks like. And it never felt like I was alone. I hope I gave him that level of confidence: that we were fine. I just feel like you can't change the past, and in that moment when someone passes away, there's nothing you can do about it. And even though it's hard, you have to forge forward.

A year later, we held a ceremony for him. We went to Florida and had a whole family thing for him and had some closure. We worked it out.

You can't repeat the cycle, especially if it's unhealthy. It's something I recognized early on. I can never make my children feel this way. The only people I care about and want approval from are my children and my wife. Those are the people I don't ever want to let down. I'm still in that phase where my kids are so young that I'm their hero, and I always want to be that person. I want them to look up to me that way. That's why I will never disrespect my wife and go fuck around and do all that shit. I don't want my kids to be like, "Wow, man. My dad was a fucking cheater. He was a fucking addict. He wasn't loyal. That's the shit my dad was."

It felt like shit to think that way, and I never want my children to feel that. I'm on a path to ensure they never feel that way about their dad. That's my fucking life mission. I'm taking all this bad stuff and learning how to learn from it, grow from it, and not repeat the cycle.

The last time I saw my uncle, we were spreading my dad's ashes in Florida. Then a couple of months later, he died from just letting his health go to shit and not taking care of himself. I'm just like, what the fuck, man? These are people who *should* be in my life, but they just went down destructive paths.

My dad became a fucking drug addict, something he would never admit to us to his dying day. We tried to help him, but there's only so many times you can do that before you have to cut someone off. I tried and tried and tried and he wouldn't be honest with me. I just had to cut him off. He didn't come to my wedding. He never met my son, and he died right around my son's first birthday. It reached a point where I thought, I can't help him—*he's* supposed to help *me* now. I can't be a dad to him when he won't go to therapy, won't get sober, all this shit. I had to cut my own dad out of my life. To this day, I don't have any regrets about it. I'm at peace with it.

12
THE BEA(S)T WITHIN

My love for electronic music started with the '90s explosion of groundbreaking groups like The Prodigy, Chemical Brothers, and Fat Boy Slim. Around that same time, I began frequenting a lot of the underground house music and techno clubs in New York City. All of it blew my mind because, well, it's all about beats.

I started using electronics in my early cover bands and still do to this day. I started working with electronic bands right after high school, and then when I moved to California, I got a gig with Krewella. That was the first time I toured the world playing EDM festivals. Krewella was merging rock with electronica, and I witnessed firsthand the energy and how the music was going over with the crowd in a truly incredible way. Then I started working with Kayzo, becoming his musical director and putting together a massive stage tour culminating in him headlining the Coachella festival's EDM Stage.

Through all of this, I was inspired to create my own music and started releasing singles with a lot of these great EDM artists. I've collaborated on EDM tracks with Virtual Riot, Modestep, Ray Volpe, and Grabbitz. I released my debut solo single, "The Less We Know," co-written and produced by Kayzo, which was recorded mere hours after my second son, Riot, was born.

I think the first time people would have seen me in an electronic context was when I was playing with Dhani Harrison. There's a significant electronic-hybrid element in his work: rock music infused with bits of electronic music. I was playing a lot of sampled drums live on pads. I would say that even though it's not EDM music, it was probably the first project that really merged electronics and rock music for me, which led to my work with Krewella.

After thenewno2 got off their tour cycle, their front-of-house and monitor engineers went on to work with Krewella. When Krewella said, "We want to add a drummer," both those guys were like, "We got the guy for you. We just got off the road with Dhani Harrison. Zummo is a rock drummer, but he's playing electronics and he loves dance music." I went and auditioned for the girls, who turned out to be huge Sum 41 fans. That was the first time everything really merged, and then I was out playing hardcore EDM festivals all over the world with Krewella, using both electronic and acoustic drums. I also infused that vibe into Sum 41 when I joined the band, and they were open and receptive to it. Long story short, Dhani Harrison and thenewno2 was the first time I brought electronics into a mainstream situation. Playing with Krewella set me on the EDM drummer path.

You know, there have been so many DJs who bring in rock drummers to capture the live energy of rock drumming. I've played numerous festivals with The Prodigy over the past decade, or actually longer—probably the past 15 years. They have a drummer now, and he's playing straight acoustic drums. There's no pads or electronics.

While I've always wanted to be a rock drummer, I also wanted to merge those electronic elements because there're certain parts in songs where it doesn't make sense to play acoustic drums. Instead of just sitting there and letting the computers handle those parts, I'd ask for samples, loops, and sounds so I could physically play them on pads. When done correctly, you can achieve a special kind of dynamic that is both exciting to hear and thrilling to watch in a live setting.

I want to point out that this all goes back to Tommy Lee when he started doing this kind of music. He was at the forefront of triggers and electronics when he was doing Methods of Mayhem. That stuff completely blew my mind because it was so sick, with those beats... and hearing those electronic sounds! It's always been part of my world, from my cover band days when I was playing straight electronic kits, or when my first acoustic kit was triggered with electronics because we were playing bars. I would say Tommy was definitely the guy who really got me excited about it, because I saw a drummer actually using this stuff to his advantage. Electronics have always been a part of my life, because I enjoy going the extra mile to play those sounds live and not rely on backing tracks, which, to me, is the lazy way. People go to a live show to see me play these parts, not have me sit there and let the machines do it. It's been a part of my DNA really forever. I think it all comes from the love of growing up with dance music, funk, and rhythmic grooves.

The first time I went to a big club in New York City, I went to a legendary club called The Tunnel. Junior Vasquez was DJing, and I stood in the middle of the floor, hearing house music through a PA in this massive room—and it was life-changing. Experiencing this music in such an amazing club and seeing people go insane had such an impact on me at 17 or 18 years old.

My association with Kayzo stemmed from, believe it or not, Sum 41. He had his birthday party at the Palladium; it was his biggest sellout show in LA. I knew someone in his crew, and he told me, "Hey, Kayzo's a huge Sum fan. Are you available for this show? Are you and Deryck available? If you guys are free, you could get up onstage and do something with him." So Deryck and I were like, "Yeah, we're down."

Deryck and I got onstage and played three Sum 41 songs (not remixes), and in between those songs, I stayed onstage with him and drummed along to his original tunes and he freaked out. It was the first time he had ever had a live drummer, and he told me backstage that "when this gets to a point where I can bring out a live band or drummer, we're gonna do this together. We're going to build something epic."

And a couple of years later, we did it. He and I built it together, and we did a headlining tour of Canada and America, eventually headlining Coachella. Instead of having keyboard players and guitarists, he wanted to have an army of drummers. I was like, "Well, I've got all these drummers I work with in Street Drum Corps." It was a unique position, because with Kayzo and Krewella, the set list changes for every single show.

There's always new music out, new remixes, whatever it may be. I knew I had to get the top drummers who could actually chart music and learn and adapt on the fly. I also wanted to bring in a group of my drummers who had never done anything with original bands at this level in their career, the ones who had been leaders for me in my various Street Drum Corps teams. It was a really cool way to give back, and I knew they would deliver. So, I drummed the whole show onstage, and then we had all these other awesome drummers come in and out throughout the performance. It really was cool and something different and exciting for that space.

The Kayzo experience inspired me to start making my own music and led to collaborations with other huge DJ artists. I've had success with Virtual Riots and Ray Volpe, being featured on singles we've written together where we added my live drums to their songs.

I met DJ/producer Jauz at (where else) a Sum 41 show, coincidentally at the Palladium in Hollywood. When Sum sold out the venue, Kayzo's manager was there and said, "I want to introduce you to Jauz." So, again, Sum is his favorite band. His wife took him to the show for his birthday as a gift, blindfolded him, walked him into the venue, and when he took off the blindfold, boom, we were his surprise birthday presents. Kayzo's manager wanted to make his birthday even more memorable by introducing him to the band.

By this point, I had been working on my first solo record, the three-song EP, *It's My War*, featuring contributions from Landon Tewers of The Plot in You, The Underclassmen, and emo-vocalist dying in designer. And then… COVID happens. We're trying to secure a label for the release, but my entire team tells me record deals are not going to happen now; no one's spending money. And while I did actually have deals on the table from several interested labels, when the pandemic hit, they all pulled back saying the same things: "We can't spend money now," or "Things are on hold, not going to happen." My team was like, "Sorry bud, this just isn't the time for the EP."

I refused to accept that. So I go into Frank mode where it's like: *How do we make this happen? What do we do?* I start thinking about how many DJs have their own record labels. That's just the way it works in this culture: They release music when they want, they put out their homies' music, all that stuff. So I remembered that I met this guy Jauz, who has his own record label called Bite This! I reached out to a mutual friend and said, "Hey, can you link me with Jauz or his team? I want to send him these demos I have and see if he's interested in putting them out."

They linked us, and he said he was in right away. Mission accomplished, and we put out the EP during COVID. I went on a writing rampage and worked with so many great artists. The following year, we ended up releasing six singles after my EP. I had a great run with Jauz; he really believed in it. We did music videos like a band would do—an anomaly in the EDM world, as they typically don't do music videos. Jauz truly believed in it, supported it, and invested money to help get this thing off the ground. I will always respect and love him for giving me a chance when nobody else would in that dark COVID time.

My immersion into EDM is anything but temporary. I also pivoted during COVID to create a live experience to promote the EP and establish a new level of artistic expression. I went into a soundstage and crafted a livestream experience where my drums were raised up in the air; I assembled a massive production and featured many guest artists. Afterward, I had a live chat with fans from all around the world.

I released an EP called *Strangers* on Kayzo's Welcome Records in 2023. Also that year, I launched a new EDM project called Gravas. I've been holding onto a special batch of songs, and when I was writing this book, it randomly came on my playlist. It literally reflected the emotions I was feeling. I quickly completed the mixes, and I'm happy to present my *Feels* EP as this book's soundtrack. To make it even more special, my sons created the single and EP art. I played them the music, and they expressed what they heard through the art.

Historically, I think it's because Sum 41 is so big and has been such a major inspiration to all of these artists. It's the wow factor, and that's the main focus. A lot of EDM artists grew up as Sum 41 fans, so I think they get fixated on that, which is fine. It's a very cool surprise to have all these roots and connections to electronic music. I've explored a lot of subgenres in this scene: drum and bass, dubstep, hardstyle… All this stuff is so fun because it's just so hype and energetic. And now with Electric Callboy, it's really fun to just play hard four on the floor for a lot of these moments in the show. It's such a stark contrast going from metal to, all of a sudden, a techno rave. It's really enjoyable for me to be able to ping-pong between those moments in the set.

I advise players of all kinds to embrace the technology. Because it's all beats at the end of the day. It's inspiring to me to play with that gear, to hear those sounds, and to create that music. I've never been negative about that because a lot of the music I like has been created that way, and that stuff sounds great. People have been going to dance clubs since day one, dancing to programmed beats. You've got a bunch of people happily dancing and being moved by that music. All the power to it, man…

Scan to listen to this book's soundtrack

13
STREET DRUM CORPSE

It was my wedding day. I'm in my suite alone, getting fixed up, dressed, and taking some time to reflect on what's about to happen. I'm also dealing with Street Drum Corps emails for all of our groups out on location. There were always things going on, which meant that there was always *work*.

That's something I've always really had to work on. I shouldn't have been dealing with any fucking emails on my wedding day. I had other people I could delegate that shit to. It was my wedding. Now, OK, I *chose* to do that, obviously. I wasn't at the altar: I was alone in my room, prior to leaving. I didn't know how to turn it off, and it's something I've had to work hard on to this day.

I don't sit there and think, "Oh man, if this fails, I'm going to look bad." That's not what it's about. Again, if I believe in something, I'm gonna go all in. I'm not doing it for the likes and comments. I don't care if people like it, but if they appreciate it, that's very nice. *I'm doing it for myself.* It's for me, for this musical outlet, this goal to help, or my love of this or that. I am all over the place with my taste in music and other projects. I need to get a lot of things out because it all completes me. I genuinely enjoy unleashing those artistic sides of myself. I don't think I could just do one thing and say, "I'm in a punk rock band! That's all I do." I love punk rock. I love metal. I love dance music. I love conducting workshops and having discussions about all of this stuff. It's everything that completes me and lets me artistically be me. And with that comes the inevitable thought: *OK, we've taken it to here. Now how do we get it to here?* It's never been an "all right, cool, we did it, let's move on" kind of thing, you know?

Unless it becomes unhealthy. Like Street Drum Corps did. It's scary walking away from something I built for almost 20 years. I've never done anything that long, only to just walk away.

The things that made money and did well—that was my expertise. I was the guy who'd send proposals to clients, and if they weren't getting back to me, I would follow up until I got an answer. I kept records of those follow-ups: what the conversation was, who was involved... I was on it. I made it my life. I really did a lot of that grueling admin work when I was on tour with Sum 41. That's what I was doing backstage and on days off. *Which cast is going where? Where's their hotel? What's the budget?*

I became everything. I was the production manager, the casting director (there's a reason why you never saw me and "Charles Einstein" in the same room at parties), the travel agent, and the business manager. When we were on tour, I would settle up the merch sales every night and divide them between the three of us. I used to put Bobby and Adam's shares in envelopes and slip them under the pillows in their bunks on the bus. (Back then, Bobby called me "Frankie Envelopes.") The experience was a lot, and it just reached a point where it wasn't worth the mental health strain or the meager financial return for all the work I was putting in.

At some point, I was like, "Guys, this is not fair. I'm doing everything. Here are all the tasks I'm handling." I think they finally agreed to give me five percent net as a manager commission, which is like two bucks at the end of the day. Net is not gross: Managers make 15 percent gross. When I finally did ask for that (not to air out dirty laundry or whatever), they said, "Absolutely not. We'd rather you teach us, and we'll learn and help you. We're not giving you the gross manager percentage."

I was just done. It just started becoming unhealthy dealing with the machine it had grown into, with all the multiple troops out there and then managing all those different personalities. I reached a point where I felt, *this isn't making me happy anymore—it's actually stressing me out*. I'm in the middle of family events, figuring out how to change this person's flight or handling this person's complaints about their hotel room, and I was just like, *what the fuck? Everything is on my plate, I'm running this whole fucking thing, and financially, it doesn't make sense anymore. And it's not fun anymore.* I just told Bobby and Adam, "I'm done. I don't want anything. I'm out. I need to move on." I still wanted to fill that void of drum shows, because I love that. After all the Interscope shit, I got us back to doing things in the parks and at fairs. That was our most successful thing—we *thrived* in it. But the amount of work required for the return on investment that we were seeing just really wasn't worth it.

We all had our roles. Mine was the theme parks and the fairs and the logistics. Bobby was the point guy for Warped and when we toured with bands, and was the band liaison when dealing with outside songwriters and label reps. Adam was our media guy and our video editor; when we had backing tracks and video images while touring, he handled all that, as well. But none of those other things were happening anymore; it was just the stuff that I was doing. So it all fell on me because that was my area of expertise. It's not their fault that there wasn't a divide-and-conquer approach that played to everyone's strengths. But when we weren't touring, and I've got 20 different fairs happening with four or five different troupes going out every weekend, it just got to be a lot.

I think when I became a dad and became responsible for two humans, that's really hard because they're my kids. My priorities just shifted; Street Drum Corps used to be my kids. All those drummers out there were like my kids. I felt like the dad making sure they got there, were checked in, and "Did you make it to this place OK?" and "How's your hotel?" When it started turning into drama—this person's fighting with that cast member, this one doesn't like the hotel room or whatever it is—I just said, "I can only be a Dad to my kids. I can't be a dad to all this anymore and bear the weight of it." I'm dealing with this all, and my partners aren't really helping, even though they said they would. I don't think they knew how. It was more stressful for me to have to teach them how to handle all this stuff and run things because I had been doing it.

But that was my expertise. It wasn't Bobby and Adam's, so I took charge. And we fucking killed it. Justin Imamura had a theme park background and was one of the first people to audition for us when we started adding cast. I took him under my wing, taught him how to tour manage, how to production manage, and threw him into the fire. Then he became one of my closest friends.

There was a situation where one of the SDC partners spoke to me in a tone that turned me off so much that it actually brought back a lot of bad memories of my Dad talking to me that way. And I was just like, *it's time for me to move on*. I'm out celebrating one of my kids' milestones at school, and I'm dealing with fucking flights and drama for one of our groups out there. This is just not healthy, and I'm doing all the heavy lifting. No one's reaching out to the other partners to address it, so it all falls on me, and if I don't take action, it's not gonna happen. Then the clients don't have a show, and we *all* lose. It's not healthy, and I'm not happy. I'd rather be friends with these guys than business partners because there's a lot of animosity that's building up here on my behalf.

I didn't want to be tied to this. I just wanted to walk away. I didn't sit down with my lawyers and ponder it. It was like, "Guys, I am out, and I don't want anything. If you guys want to keep it going, go ahead. I just need to legally detach from everything. I'm going to remove my name from the business, bank accounts, and credit cards. That was the only drama. When my lawyer drafted up my exit papers, they pushed back and insisted I sign a non-compete contract for a bunch of years. My lawyer told them, "You have no grounds because Frank is not receiving a payout. He's walking away. He can do whatever he wants."

I didn't get shit—I didn't *want* anything. But leaving freed me to do whatever I wanted. Because if I were to get some big cash-out, there'd be stipulations attached to that. I didn't want any conditions. I wanted to be free and clear to do whatever I wanted—and money wouldn't provide me that freedom. So I walked.

Street Drum Corps tried our hands at so much. The Interscope thing was technically a failure, but I see it as an education. And it did give me the money to get my own apartment and do the things I was struggling to do. After all this hype and all this money spent, we made records, but nothing ever came out, and we got dropped. (Interestingly enough, the first person I saw when I got offstage on the first day of the When We Were Young festival was Louis Bandak, our A&R guy at Interscope during that time; haven't seen or spoken to him since then).

It reached a point where I was like, "OK, we've done everything." I mean, even our Hard Rock Vegas residency looked like a success on paper, but filling that fucking room was the hardest thing we ever had to do. Some nights, we only had half of the house filled, and they were ready to cancel our residency. We had special guests like Tommy Lee and Deryck Whibley, but Hard Rock was gonna cancel our last show. Then suddenly, they thought, "Oh hey, Nine Inch Nails is playing in the big room in the casino. You guys are here. You know what? Fuck it: Let's blow this out. Let's make your show free for everyone after the Nails show." So we ended on a high note, but they didn't see the profits they wanted. It wasn't really a success business-wise. Much of what we did just felt like constantly fighting to do the next thing. Like, if we hadn't had the theme parks and fairs going, we wouldn't have been able to fund all that stuff. I didn't earn a single dollar doing the residency in Vegas; we had fucking stilt walkers and a backing band and all of these mounting expenses. Without these groups out there doing the Halloween shows, the fairs, and the theme parks, we wouldn't have been able to pull off the passion project stuff. It looked like a success, but much of it really wasn't.

We just went with it all because in Street Drum Corps, there were no rules. It was this avant-garde art project, but if we had stayed in one lane and really focused, I feel like it could have been incredibly successful. And it was really fucking hard work. At a certain point, it wasn't financially stable enough—that's why I had to hustle with other things. I learned a lot because we did a hell of a lot.

Bobby and Adam are still doing a couple shows a year, whatever they can, but it's not what it used to be. Bobby owns a pizzeria, and Adam has a full-time job in IT. They've got families now, so they do SDC more for fun whenever they can to just get their rocks off performing, since they're not in bands or anything. So yeah, SDC is still a thing, for sure.

After Street Drum Corps was over and done, I had an idea. I told Justin, "We enjoy this. Let's fucking truly reinvent the game. Let's do something where we're completely ghosts..."

14
THE DRUMHEADS

The person who helped me the most during Street Drum Corps was our secret/not secret/not official partner Justin Imamura. He wasn't an on-paper partner in SDC, but we compensated him equally out of goodwill. He was on the West Coast, dealing with all the NorCal groups at theme parks and fairs while I dealt with the SoCal groups. Later on, I would oversee the East Coast Halloween shows, and he managed middle America and the West Coast. We'd have a conference call once a week to go through it all, splitting up the training for the different casts on the road. Without him, I wouldn't've been able to manage it.

So when Street Drum Corps was dead and done for me, I realized that I really enjoyed being in business with Justin. We complemented each other equally: It wasn't like I was doing 25 percent and he was doing 75 percent. This was a solid 50-50 partnership. I started to think, *there's gotta be more to offer in this world than what we're offering.* While I had been out doing all those fairs and gigs, I was taking notice.

I noticed that the things that were going over the biggest were costume characters that little kids would just run to, and shows onstage featuring songs that people know. And I was like, *how do you combine those elements and add the drumming because, obviously, we're drummers.* I was literally standing at a urinal when it hit me: "Oh, my God: It's a drum show! Make the character an actual drumhead! And these drumhead characters that can perform all this fun kid stuff. It's like a dance party drum show! They're costume characters. Just blend it all together." I shared the idea with Justin. We came up with a list of really popular songs that kids love, along with some classics. We sketched this out in one afternoon and started getting quotes.

The thing that people love in the world of theme parks and fairs is costume characters and stage shows with songs people know. What I had been observing is that the clientele of fairs and theme parks mainly consists of country folks and a lot of Latinos. Let's give them what they want! Let's give them country music, let's give them Latino music, let's give them popular kids' music. We put it all together so fucking quickly and went and showcased it.

Fast-forward a year, we were showcasing it. We invested all of our money into this whole endeavor equally. We think it's rad. We had our kids watch rehearsals, and they thought it was rad. But we go to a convention showcase where it's either gonna sink or swim. The vibe at the showcase was a big convention, WFA, in Reno, where fair entertainment acts put it out there. We watched it: band, band, band, band… and people were not into it. They were starting to leave.

We had the last spot. We're on last, which was not good. We come out, and the place erupts. People start running back, and we have a freaking conga line happening. The next day at our booth, there's a line, and we're booked solid for next summer—this thing is off and running. It's a hit, and it just keeps getting bigger and bigger.

We had custom headgear made that were literally 14-inch toms with a character face on them. We've got a giant inflatable blow-up onstage of the character. Everything is red, white, and blue, as Americana as you can get, because that's what fairs are. The first residency we did in March was a 10-day run in deep, deep Southern California—practically in Mexico in El Centro. We did a show for special needs kids. They bussed in senior citizens and kids who were deaf, blind, had Down syndrome, you name it. We filled the whole theater because this is a stage show. It's been on all the main stages of all the fairs we've done. And everybody's in there, and you can see all the challenges these kids face, like being fixated on something.

The second we went on, suddenly no one seemed to have a disability. The music swept through the crowd with emotion and joy. And then during the portion where we invite audience members onstage to drum? To be that close to joy… Thank God I had a costume head on. It takes a lot for me to cry, but I lost it. It was just so powerful to witness, the joy that music brings to people. This is why I do music like this. I am reminded that without music, I'd be fucked, you know?

The first shows were in March 2023, and we could only do those shows when I was off the road with Sum, so we just booked what I could do. We did eight state and county fair residencies in California, from Southern to NorCal. We just wrapped 12 shows, and it's gnarly! We're wearing full jumpsuits because the characters are non-binary: You can't tell if there's a man or woman or what race. We're covered from head to toe, and we want it to be that way. So we're fully suited up, drumming, and it's been 100-and-something degrees at most of the shows we've done this summer. Talk about being put to the test. It's just another creative venture that launched this year.

We put it in front of the public, and people went nuts! We've been booked this whole year, and the joy it's bringing to special needs kids is completely amazing! Our kids love it, and who knows, maybe they can have this one day or talk about building a completely different business from their own ideas and seeing it in action within a year?

It's a 25-minute show. I built a DJ mix of popular music from kids' songs to classic hits. Half the show we're drumming, interacting with the audience and bringing kids onstage. And then for the second half, it's a meet-and-greet dance party where we engage with the crowd, bringing all the kids and parents up for a full-on dance party. Everyone who attends describes it as "a kids rave." It's so fun.

Why do we do it? Justin and I both have two sons, all close in age. They come out to the shows, and the joy of them being at a fair is wonderful, all the fun that it is. I took my boys for the first time for eight days without my wife. They were with me at the same fair, seeing the same show. By the eighth day, they were just as excited as on the first day. My kids get to be part of this. Maybe they'll want to take over this business one day. It's really cool. Drumheads fulfills my love of drum shows and theme parks. It's me and one other person, and we handle *everything*. No one else is involved. We do it per our availability, and it's not going to be a machine.

The show was so well-received that state and county fairs have offered us contracts for the next two years. I've never had that in my career! It's always been year to year. But apparently, it's the hottest show in the fair world… Honestly, we're not even touring it: We're just staying local in Northern California. I did all of them, except for one four-day residency because I was out with Sum, so I had to find someone to take over for me. But we're not going to turn this into some deployment scheme, enlisting a ton of troops and all that, because that's when things get fucked and this show is too custom. You've got to know how to be a costume character, a drummer, a dancer, and be able to work well with kids. It's basically Justin and I just being corny dads up there because we have kids of our own and we know what to do. It's both rad and rewarding.

We go in and do residencies at elementary schools. It's something so much greater and more heartfelt than Street Drum Corps ever was to me because it provides such a deep, special joy. The joy it brings and what it offers in this space… You don't see stuff like that. It's pretty incredible.

Here's the thing: I don't promote the Drumheads. I don't post about it. It exists where it exists: You see it there. I don't need the recognition. We were in the dressing room for a show at the last fair of the year. I haven't been able to perform a lot of the shows because I've been on the road with Sum. So we hired and trained someone to play with Justin (who, by the way, was killing it). Backstage, it came out that I hadn't been at this fair previously because I was on tour. Somehow it came out, and they were asking, "Oh, what band are you in?" And I was like, "Uh, it's on my son's shirt."

Their jaws dropped when they found out that this guy putting on a costume head (which I actually wore as a cameo in the Sum 41 video for "Rise Up" on our current album, because the guys just thought it was amazing) was actually in a well-known band. But it exists where it exists. The Drumheads are costume characters. You don't know who it is. I don't need to boast about it. And most people reading this book are going to hear about this for the first time. What I love about Drumheads gigs is that I put on that head and no one knows it's Frank Zummo. I don't exist.

Here's a story: At one of the most recent fairs I missed because I was on tour, Street Drum Corps was actually there—and sharing the same dressing room with the Drumheads. It was fine: It wasn't the owners. They sent out a cast, but Justin knows them all very well, and they were just shocked to see him. And he's like, "Yeah, this is what I do now." I wasn't there, so it didn't turn into something, you know, dramatic like it could have. So I'm glad I wasn't there so we could avoid any potential unnecessary drama. But yeah, that was pretty funny—which is cool. Both groups are still getting booked at the same events. Great for everyone. Everybody wins, right?

15

BEING A BETTER... EVERYTHING

Driving four hours after playing a huge rock show is truly a grind. But it's about showing up and being here for these kids and giving them a workshop experience. The wellness training I do is a whole other chapter because everyone's like, "Oh, you're the machine."

This is how I do it: I'm in the pool doing training with weights, where I have to hold my breath. Dave Brownsound [Baksh, Sum 41 guitarist] and I did that in North Carolina on a day off. We drove two hours away to train with one of Laird Hamilton's coaches. It's a constant quest for me: How can I sustain better? How can I do this more effortlessly? I'm on this ongoing journey, a constant quest to be as healthy as I can.

Like I said previously, I never really got the hang of meditation. My mind would wander to other things. When I started studying breathwork, it was the first time I actually felt my body getting a reset. As I do it, I'm connecting with myself and just focusing on breath. It was the first thing that really changed the game for me on such an impactful level.

And how funny is that? Because breathing is what we do to survive. But I learned so much about it when I was at the bottom of a pool and couldn't breathe. At first, it was a very scary place. You panic. You think you're going to drown; the fear is at such a level. This summer was the first time I was in the pool at the home of one of Laird Hamilton's coaches. I was 12 feet deep at the bottom of the pool, then all of a sudden, I thought, *Wow, I'm at peace here. It feels really good.* I finally found my peace within the water, just holding my breath, and it was pretty incredible. Five years into this journey, I finally felt comfortable and at peace in the water after doing those insane workouts.

All the prep work is great. I started doing all these insane things like the cold plunges and the recovery and the sauna and the workouts and—just everything. I think it's changed me as a human, and hopefully, it's making me a better spouse and a father.

One of my breathwork coaches (who has been a huge savior for me) taught me how to use breath to down-regulate; to up-regulate before I go on stage (instead of having coffee); and to get fired up for a show. That same breath coach is a therapist, and I've never had a therapist in my life. I just started talking to her about finding balance, trying to be a better human, and growing to be a better husband and dad. Just everyday life stuff, too, and my way of dealing and the work that I'm doing on it.

People always ask, "What's your hobby?" It's wellness, because that's what I can count on. That's what I spend my time doing and researching. Of course, nothing beats the show. I used to party and have fun, just not at a toxic level. I'm 100% sober on tour. I'll enjoy a glass of wine with my wife for special events—that's it. No drugs, nothing. But right when I got in Sum and saw how hard this band goes and how I'm the driving force behind it, there was no fucking around.

We're never too old to learn. And I'm not ashamed to acknowledge and learn and to better myself as a human. I feel like that's something we can get across, too. Like, put your fucking ego and your macho-dude bullshit aside, dude. My dad was a super Italian macho guy, and I don't want to be that. I definitely want to grow, learn, and just be a better partner and father.

There's that great comedian, Bert Kreischer, who found success later in life and is so appreciative of it. He never wants it to go back to the way it was. That's why he's touring and grinding more than any comedian. It's so relatable to me. There's a word everyone likes to use these days: "longevity." I went on a wellness journey, a deep dive over the past 10 years, in the quest for longevity for my career and my family.

Now I'm getting hit up by everybody. "Hey, how do I do the ice bath?" or "How well does the sauna work?" I feel like I'm a health guru for so many drummers and musicians. Sum's former security guy just called me and said the drummer he's working for on tour is having problems, asking, "What do I do?" I always start with, "Well, this is what works for me. You can start there and then see how he feels." But it's cool that I'm getting known as this health guy. Everybody thinks I'm a vegan because it's so healthy, and they assume that. I'm actually not. I just eat really organic, raw, and well.

Let's go back a bit. I'm about to go on the longest tour I've ever done in my life, nine weeks in Europe with Sum 41. I'm leaving Lauren and my son Brixton who has just turned one. Before I leave, writer Neil Strauss invites me to be on his podcast, *The Truth Barrel*. Co-hosted by Strauss and pro-volleyball player/podcast host Gabby Reece, the premise of the podcast is that you're stuck in a 200-and-something degree sauna doing an interview in your board shorts. That's where I met Gabby, and it changed my life in every way before I went on the nine-week tour.

She gave me health tips, and I left her house with bags of different powders and supplements. Anytime I would have a question, I could call her. Gabby and her husband, surfing legend Laird Hamilton, even invited me to Hawaii.

I got a personal trainer right when I turned 30. I was like, *I don't know how to work out. I go to the gym, but I don't know what the fuck I'm doing. I'm gonna get a trainer to learn how to work out properly, to push me.* So I just went to a gym, got a personal trainer, and did CrossFit shit from, like, 30 onward. But when I met Gabby and Laird, that's when I got taken on this journey that I'm still on to this day.

I started feeling way overwhelmed. Shit was getting out of control mentally for me, so I called my therapist. I also worked with our girl who's on tour with us, who teaches yoga and meditation. And I started doing things to help clear my plate and learn coping mechanisms. Back in the day, I would just be like, *push that shit in the basement, keep going, keep going. It's weak, no weakness.* But now I get it—if you put that shit into the basement, one day it's gonna fucking explode, and it's gonna be really bad. So I have to keep that basement empty.

There's also that reminder that I can say no, knowing it's not worth my family or my mental capacity to go do this one extra fucking show, you know? I need to practice what I preach to these kids when we're playing the What's on Your Plate game. Coping mechanisms have helped me so much in having these conversations and finding different ways to cope. In the last couple of years, I've really acknowledged this stuff and realized I can change my whole approach. I used to be like, "I don't fucking need therapy! I'm OK! Everything's good! Just fucking power through, macho man!" No, that actually *isn't* OK, so I'm restructuring everything. The takeaway is I don't want to ever be in a dark place because I've let things build up. So whatever I have to do to stay healthy, discuss things, have conversations, and seek help, I will do.

We definitely live in a much healthier world now. I mean, I'm sure you get sick of looking through your social media feeds and seeing every fucking artist in an ice bath doing cold plunges or hanging out at the gym. It's trendy, but it's a cool trend because focusing on your health in general helps your mental well-being too. It was great when I joined Sum 41 and I was blessed to meet these amazing athletes and people who changed my whole perspective.

I cut out alcohol from touring, just to be clear. Everybody in a band is always like, "Yeah, I need a drink before I go on to take the edge off." I was that person, and I did my first show in Japan with Krewella for the first time in a million years without having that drink before the show. And the fucking adrenaline! I was so jacked; it was a feeling I hadn't felt in so long. I was like, *why have I been taking that away? I want this edge! This is like fucking rocket fuel, and it's amazing*!

I went to Hawaii for Laird Hamilton's XPT experience. It's a three-day retreat where you're doing pool training with weights, ice baths, and saunas, and you're out in nature doing workouts and all this other stuff. I went right before the pandemic. We did guided breathwork with Laird for 30 or 45 minutes. And holy shit, when you actually focus and learn how to use it to down-regulate, get amped, activate, or just reset, it flipped me upside down and completely changed my life.

Now this is crazy, because I never believed in this type of stuff, ever, but I had an out-of-body experience doing breathwork. When we were done, I ran over to Laird and I was like, "Dude, when we were doing this, I saw my body go float into the sky. I was looking at myself and then I came back down. What the fuck is going on?" He replied, "That's normal."

It happens when you go there with breathwork, and it's emotional. You cry like, "Shit, I didn't even know that was in me." Honestly, it was the best thing I could have learned before the pandemic. I taught it to my family and do it with my kids when they're all wound up and can't settle down for bedtime or fall asleep. I'm teaching this to my kids, but I didn't learn it until I was… fucking 40 years old. I do it with some of the Sum 41 guys to get amped up before a show. I do it every night before bed, because you're lying there with your thoughts, like, "What am I gonna do tomorrow?" Breathwork puts me to bed. It lets me focus on breathing instead of "What do I got to do when I wake up." I truly believe it's the number one thing you can do for your mental health. It really is so important, and I'm trying to spread that message because it changed my fucking life.

There's great behind-the-scenes footage of my music video "E.O.T.E. (Edge of the Earth)" where I'm playing drums at the bottom of their pool. We had to put dumbbells in the drums to keep them from floating up. While I'm in Laird and Gabby's pool, I'm wearing a weight belt so I wouldn't float up—which is kinda scary, you know? We added a subliminal element to the video that I'm sure nobody caught, but I don't care—it's for me. Laird reaches his hand into the pool when I'm fighting under the water, as if to say, "You're not gonna drown." I'm freaking out, and there's a hand that comes into the water, and you see through this reflection a man who pulls me out of the water. That was Laird.

I included it in the music video because this guy gave me a rebirth of life in a way, really. Him bringing me into his world, teaching me all these techniques, and introducing me to all these people—it just gave me a whole new life, and I wanted to put that in the video as a little subliminal nod to him.

LAIRD HAMILTON AND GABRIELLE REECE, creators and founders of XPT Life extreme performance training:

GABRIELLE REECE: I think Frank was at a place where he realized that he wanted to make a change in order to stay high performance. Drumming, obviously, is highly physical, and he reached out to us because he was trying to find ways to develop new tools to support him on the road. So he came to Hawaii the first time for XPT, where there is breathing, but there's also pool training and heat and ice. So we developed a relationship that way.

LAIRD HAMILTON: We have a program, XPT, that we do a couple times a year, bringing in a big group of people. Frank got wind of that, and then he participated in that program. From that opportunity, we developed a friendship.

At first, I didn't fully appreciate how athletic Frank is. You don't think of musicians as athletes. I mean, drumming is obviously an athletic activity, but Frank's particular type of drumming is on another level. When I saw him play, I think that's when I really could appreciate everything it was taking for him to maintain that level—he's not stereotypical. I know that's changed a lot in the industry over the years, but normally you don't equate musicians with athletes. But, they are today, especially the older ones, because they want to sustain their performance. They've realized, "The only way I'm going to continue to do this is to take care of myself." I appreciate his humility, which is something I gravitate towards when I see somebody who's great at what they do, and then they're open and wanting to learn.

REECE: It's easy to admire and appreciate Frank. He's gentle, but he's a sweet person. But then he's just savage. That is really a fun combination, where you have this person who's no bullshit and really direct and really dedicated to what they're doing, but also really kind and sweet.

HAMILTON: I think someone who's already at that level of performance already does so many things correctly. Sometimes they just need a sounding board. If you're alone out there and everybody else is doing a different thing, and then you meet people that maybe have a similar philosophy or are doing a similar thing, it can confirm your suspicions. I believe that he was already internally exploring it. Once you're doing the right thing, you know when you're doing the wrong thing. You know what's working, so you know when it doesn't work. When you are alone in that, I think it's more difficult because maybe all those other influences aren't supportive, and then you meet other people that can confirm some of your suspicions. Maybe they have a couple little tricks they've learned from other people. I feel like we're always just passing on what we've learned from other people, too. So, if we're at all useful to Frank, it's just because we've shared the things that have been useful for us. But again, I think to have that sounding board to go and say, "OK, you're on the right track," or "Yeah, that makes sense."

REECE: Laird is still deeply in pursuit of his sport, and so, for Frank, it's like, "Oh, I can do the thing I love at a very high level for a really long time." I think Laird definitely reminded Frank of that—the way that Laird is and his approach to training and dealing with challenges.

I think Frank is a pretty emotionally balanced person, and I think that he can sense when something is going to become a problem or isn't going to work for him. So I think he was looking for ways to deal with it long before he was in the mania of "I'm desperate and I'm underwater." Also, Laird's from Hawaii, I'm from the Caribbean—we're not really from Southern California. So I think there's a sort of understood energy that, when we all get together, we're all just going to be here to work hard and learn and be humble. Besides, people don't really survive the environment that they're in or that they put other people in if they *don't* come with humility.

Those are the things that, you know, those are the commonalities amongst all the people who can sustain a certain level of output over a long period of time.

HAMILTON: We have our own problems with the kind of training we're doing, never mind beating a drum. [*Laughs.*] Breathwork is always profound. It's always profound because we all breathe. Since Frank is a cardio monster, he's so in touch with his breath. His breath is part of his work. And if he can't breathe right and breathe well, then his work is going to be affected. So someone like that is obviously going to have a much more profound effect with breathwork than somebody else who does things where the breathing isn't such a critical part. I think that's why the breathwork was profound to him. It usually is when you deal with people that are so connected to their breath already. He's so connected with his breath because the rhythm, his breathing, his breath is all in cadence with his drumming. Normally, we just speed up our breathing when we need more, when we have more activity, and we slow it down we have less activity. So in a way, it can be a lot more structured than that, and I think he appreciates that.

REECE: It leads to two really common themes for Frank. One is how much he really loves what he does. I think his commitment to his craft is deep and wide. The other part of that is to his family. "How can I be the best husband or dad? How can I provide for my family and teach them good habits? So really all of this actually just points arrows to: this guy loves what he does, he takes his craft very seriously—and then obviously his relationship with his family is what that means to him.

HAMILTON: I appreciate that he drums well, but being a good dad? There's fewer of those than there are good drummers. Frank understands that he can have an influence, and if you're fortunate to be in that position, then you are obligated. The rarity we have in our world is that the people who are in positions of influence don't take it as a responsibility for the positive.

I admire any time somebody is in pursuit of sustained mastery, right? Because there's mastery and then there's sustained mastery. Mastering something is one thing, but sustaining mastery over a long period of time is much more difficult. I always liked the idea of victory through attrition, where you're the last guy standing. I just think Frank is that kind of guy, the kind of guy where everybody's going to fall away and he's still going to be in there doing it. And he's probably going to meet some other younger guys to join him.

REECE: It's not being about great, it's about being great *for a long time.* That takes a different thing.

RESOURCES

Wellness Management:
XPT Life (app, events: xptlife.com)
Supplements:
Laird Superfood (lairdsuperfood.com)
ORGANIXX (shop.organixx.com)
Primal Kitchen (primalkitchen.com)
Hardware:
Nordic Sauna (nordicsauna.com)
Plunge (plunge.com)

Books:
Kristen Ulmer's *The Art of Fear*
Laird Hamilton's *Liferider*
Rick Rubin's *The Creative Act: A Way of Being*
James Nestor's *Breath*
Timothy Gallwey's *The Inner Game of Tennis*
Darin Olien's *Fatal Conveniences*

16
SPECIAL BEAT SERVICE

This is our final two-week tour of the year, and the last time we're hitting Australia. We're headlining a three-city festival, then it's home for the holidays. After that, just one tour left: Canada. And then… we're done. It's getting real in every way.

You know what else is real? Jet lag. The flight from Paris to Brisbane is something like 21 hours, and jet lag is a fucking *beast*. I'm 30 minutes from soundcheck when management texts me, saying we're canceling tonight's show. Deryck has pneumonia. And the rest of the tour might be canceled, depending on what the doctors say tomorrow. I didn't even know he was feeling sick. I hadn't seen him since we landed.

Immediately we realize we've come all the way to the other side of the world; we're here, headlining festivals; there's no making up dates on a final tour; this is the last time in every city; and it's not like we'll get another shot on a Final Tour. It was just so devastating, in every way.

As I'm sitting there, bummed and dark with emotions, grandson calls me. He was on the festival bill, but for all our headlining arena shows, he was our opening act. So he calls and he's like, "Dude, this really sucks, but I'm here. I'm doing a free pop-up show tonight at a little venue I found. Will you come drum with me on my big song to end the set? And I don't have an opening act—will you DJ and open the show? All these kids are lined up outside the venue. It's a free show. Let's do something. Let's rally."

Me? I was like, "I'm in, dude."

I learned "Blood // Water" quickly and prepped a DJ set. (Good thing I had my USBs with me.) I raced down to the venue, soundchecked with grandson, and literally went right on stage and kicked off the night with a DJ set. It was packed. Everyone was stoked to be there and see us perform, in light of the cancellation. And it got my gears going. *OK, I've come this far. I need to do something. I need to do something while I'm here.* The band is still in limbo, unsure of what's happening with the dates. Our return flights take off from Sydney, so we had to get there, and all our flights and hotels were non-refundable anyway. Deryck's staying in

Brisbane; management says he can't fly with his lungs and pneumonia. But they also tell us that "the rest of you guys are going to have to carry on until we figure out exactly how to get you all home."

I had a School of Rock workshop planned in Sydney for the next week, so I moved it a week earlier. Dan Kerby, who's my dear drumming friend, said, "Hey man, let me link you with Drumtek. It's the biggest drum shop in Australia, let's see if we can do a workshop." Got on the phone with them, and they planned a last-minute workshop event with me. So OK, at least I did this DJ set and some guest drumming with grandson and two workshops. I'm making the most of my time here. So we leave Brisbane and go to Melbourne.

Today is the first festival day that we've now canceled. I get to the hotel and I start seeing all the bands at the festival in the lobby. And now it just hit me: *This really sucks.* We're not playing this festival. All the emotions and bummed-outness just kicked in on another level because that's when it got real for me. And I was beyond jet-lagged. I wasn't sleeping well. I got some dinner and then I went to bed. The last thing I texted Lauren before I went to bed was something like, "I'm really bummed now, seeing all the bands here and the festival's tomorrow and this really sucks." I went to bed and thankfully slept through the night. I got over my jet lag, woke up at 6 a.m. and I was just like, "I'm gonna turn this around today. I'm going to go to the gym and have a good workout."

I'm finishing up my workout when I get a text from Sum 41's tour coordinator. She's like, "Where are you? I need to talk to you, right *now.*" I'm thinking, *are you fucking kidding me*? What else could be wrong? Like what? It sounded like it was going to be something serious.

So she shows up at the gym and asks me, "Hey, so you know the band Electric Callboy?"

Absolutely.

"They're taking your spot in the festival headlining," she continues. "Now their drummer has to go home, and they're about to cancel. The festival is gonna lose the band that replaced you, too. The tour manager asked if a) you're still in the country—because they know you guys canceled but weren't sure if you left—and b) would you be interested in talking to the guys about potentially filling in tonight?"

I didn't even hesitate. I'm in; I love this band. I play their songs in my DJ sets. Whatever they need, I got this. Let's set up a meeting. She says, "OK, the guys are still asleep. It's all being figured out."

I go to breakfast, and then I get a call: "Hey, come to the lobby. Band management, tour management, everyone's here. We need to have a meeting." I head down to meet the guys, and they hit me with the situation. "It's now like 10, 10:30 in the morning. Can you learn our hour set and play it tonight at 7:30 p.m.?" They're freaking out, feeling like "We don't even deserve to take Sum 41's spot, and now this shit happens." They were really stressed out.

I just said, "My tech is here, he wants to work. Let me send him to deal with the drums so I can just focus on learning the parts. And I'll send our band assistant to handle the rest". Again, it was all about giving me some time to learn the songs. My team trained their team since mine was only there for the first two shows, then their crew took over. As for the money? Their manager just said, "Here's my email, send me an invoice." That was it—no bullshit like, "Call my manager, he'll call my attorney, who will call my agent, and we'll get back to you." If I were in this situation, I'd hope others would step up. I'm just wired to react positively, in a way that's gonna help the whole situation.

And it was awesome. Because I hadn't done this in ages. You know, I used to do it a lot with Mötley and Scott Weiland and stuff like that, but it had been a minute. They literally sent me a set list. I only knew two songs, but I didn't *know* them, so I charted everything out. Went to the gig, same deal: no soundcheck, no rehearsal, never even sat behind the drum set since it wasn't my kit, I just went up there. And it was insane.

This is how I kicked off my workshop at Drumtek in Melbourne. I walked into the room and said, "Before I play for you guys, let me tell you why I'm even here." I wanted to get everybody amped-up and drop a life lesson right off the bat. Then I launched into a 15-minute medley. Then we pulled kids from the crowd to join in and play a little. Some didn't know the songs—they'd just heard them. It was awesome. We had pulled seven kids from the audience, and it was really cool. There were fans there, too, who were stoked to meet me and get their records signed and stuff because they didn't get to see Sum at the festival. It felt great to be able to just rally and do something meaningful. Plus, it was amazing to be able to make phone calls and have supportive people in a country I don't even live in and have only visited a couple of times. Just being able to call a friend and—boom!—get help setting up a drum workshop is so cool. It's a sweet spot in my career where people are like, "Yeah, you're here. Let's do it. You're going to sell tickets, and it's going to be a successful event." That kind of support is really fucking cool.

The Callboys are such a fun party band! It's dance music, but then it gets heavy, and then the pits and the jumping up and down start happening—it's amazing. I delivered for them, and the respect from the crowd was massive. When they shared the story to pay respect to Deryck and the band, we played a snippet of "Still Waiting," and the place erupted. And when they talked about me? Well, I've never heard a roar like that in my life! The festival owner was so emotional. He said, "You saved the festival! I was about to lose so much. I lost you guys, and I was going to lose your replacement. You made this whole full circle, because the Sum 41 fans have you representing. Thank you, thank you, thank you!"

So now I was in Electric Callboy, touring three cities in Australia, and each day just kept getting better and better. The whole thing blew up online: news stories and everything went viral. For me, it was incredible to be able to step in, deliver, and earn respect from both the band and the fans. Honestly, I needed that for my soul; all the insecurity about my future just vanished. I haven't felt this fire in a long time. It made me realize that I still got it and can still deliver in these situations. This experience put me on a whole other level in the industry.

I told the guys, "I hope everything is okay with your drummer." Because they've got the next two years ahead—the biggest cycle of their lives. They're headlining all the same festivals that Sum 41 played last year. It's massive: sold-out arena tours around the world, crazy stuff. I said, "Hey, If you need me, I got you. If things work out with your drummer, great, but it was an honor to be here." Their music totally fits my drumming style: dance music and metal. You know, it just makes sense.

Then I flew back to Melbourne for my fourth show in a row to do a workshop. It was last-minute: The drum shop was like, "We don't know if anyone's gonna show up." I walk into that room, and it's completely sold out, packed from front to back. Usually, in this drum shop, they do very traditional drum clinics—but I go in with my anti-clinic vibe. I went in there, did my thing, and then started pulling kids from the audience to jam with me on Sum 41 songs. It was just magical—like they always are.

Mental health questions came up. It turned into what all my workshops naturally become, organically, and being in a country where I've never held a drum workshop—plus doing it in a place that doesn't follow my usual curriculum—was such an incredible way to wrap things up. The shop thanked me for doing what I did for this community of upcoming drummers. This is exactly what it's about; this is why I do this. I came home feeling so fulfilled after turning such a negative situation into something positive.

If I'm dealt a bad card, am I gonna sit there in my hotel room and fester in negativity? Hell, no. Let's flip this bad situation. I've come this far, I'm here, and I literally put it out into the universe at the airport on my way to Melbourne. Before that canceled festival, I just put it out there. With all these bands here and everyone's getting sick and all this travel, how amazing would it be to fill in for one of these huge bands at the festival? I put it out there. And while all this was happening, my team was like, "How are you not freaking out? You're so calm." Because this is what I do; I'm always ready for these moments. I've trained my whole life for this shit. And it was cool to have that fire reignited because I haven't had to do that in a very, very long time. And it's just the most amazing and special way to end a year and set myself up for the future.

Finally, when I got back to Brisbane for the last festival, Deryck was still there. He was finally cleared to go home, and I filled him in on everything that had gone down. He was really touched that the Callboys were doing "Still Waiting" as a tribute, and about all the support, from the lowest of lows to the highest of highs in just 24 hours. I went from having nothing to do to three shows and a workshop. I gotta give props to grandson; he called me before I could even start thinking about anything. He just got me fired up and thinking, *this is exactly why we're here.*

17
THE LOUDEST GOODBYE

MIKE CIPRARI: I literally was with him in the car. I was driving and he was in the front seat after the School of Rock gig when he got notified that Sum 41's next tour was going to be their last. And the cool, calm, collected nature of Frank didn't waver. He was just thinking. I mean, holy shit, it *had* to have burned, it *had* to have felt like a gut punch. Anybody else would have punched the window, screamed, or just went, you know, "boo-hoo me." Not Frank.

It's the top of 2023 and I have just played the biggest workshop of all time in Florida. It was the most amazing show in every way. It was a packed house. The kids were just on fire: they were so amped up! The performances were incredible. At the meet-and-greet, one kid came with his head shaved like the opposite of a mohawk, like in the "Fat Lip" video; he tried to look like that girl with the inverted mohawk shave—and then he handed me clippers and asked me to shave the rest of his head! It was just a wild show. The parents were asking questions, and we had amazing conversations.

That was actually the first show where we brought along SPTS (Society for the Prevention of Teen Suicide) which is a prevention charity. That was the first time we played the game, What's on Your Plate?, where we passed out paper plates and Sharpies to the kids and asked them what major things they were thinking or worried about. That show was the first time I met the SPTS team, and they were like, "Hey, we kind of have this idea about this paper plate game, but we don't know if it's going to go over well." And I was like, "Let's go for it. Let's go break the ice with the kids first. Before we do that, let me go up there and introduce you guys, introduce myself, and then let's play this game." The game went over so well that now we do it at every one of my events when SPTS can be there. So incredible, and what a great way to start!

My phone's in my book bag backstage. I go back there and pick it up just to see what time it is. I see texts from Dave Brownsound, Cone, and Tom, all saying. "Did you see the email?" *What the fuck? Did something happen? What was going on?*

I opened my inbox, and it's this really long email Deryck sent to each one of us. To be honest, I just skimmed through it. I didn't sit down to read it because I had to go to a dinner—Mike from SJC Drums was there, and we were going to a nice dinner to celebrate. And I just glanced through it.

My take from reading it through—'cause my mind was just not in the right place, I literally read it wrong—my takeaway from just skimming through it was that Sum 41 was moving forward without me, Tom, Dave, and Cone. I thought we were all getting fired, and Deryck was gonna do the band without us.

I put my phone down, looked at it again, and realized that it was Deryck saying he feels *Heaven :x: Hell* is the best record he's ever made and it's a great way to end this band. He just can't do it anymore. He loves us all and wants to give the fans a proper way to say goodbye, so we're going on a world tour. I went into mourning, as I would a death, but I had to put on a happy face, go to dinner, and not talk about it.

The next day, I have a morning flight back home. I went to the airport and thought, *You know what? Deryck said we don't need to get back to him right away. Take time to process and call him when we're ready*. But then I was like, *You know what? I'm about to get on a plane right now. If God forbid this plane goes down and I don't tell him what I want to tell him*... I'll send an email.

I was on the runway, and the plane turns back. A storm was coming in and all flights were grounded, which honestly was a blessing because I would have gone home and been a mess. I was stuck in Florida, so I got on the phone with management and called my band members individually to talk through this. Then Deryck actually called me because of the email I sent him. We had over an hour of beautiful conversation that felt so healthy. When I picked up the phone I was mourning, and when I hung up the phone, I was so excited. It gave me clarity and closure. I went from the lowest of lows to the highest of highs because we had such great communication. And I knew I had a long time—a year and a half—to enjoy one more trip around the world.

I told Deryck that as hard as it is to understand, I respect him for wanting to go out on top. He's not going to fake it or go through the motions just to go on and be miserable. I don't want to tour with someone like that. So I commended him for being honest, as tough as it was. I also thanked him for giving me this life, my golden ticket. I have pretty much everything in my life because of Sum 41 now. It bought me my first house and provided for my family. I just thanked him for everything, for the ride of a fucking lifetime, and for giving me this chance in this band.

I told him I quit Street Drum Corps, which obviously wasn't Sum-41 level, but it just became so overwhelming that it was actually not healthy for me. I had to walk away because I do music for the joy of it, and if I'm in something and it's negative, then I'm out. If it can't be fixed or turned into a healthy place, I'm gone. I'm in a blessed position where I get to do music because it's my art, it's my passion. If it becomes a negative thing, it's time to reassess or move on.

I think it's hard for me because it went from nothing to what it is now, rebuilding this band from the ground up. The other day, the band told me this is the best US tour they've ever done with the most ticket sales and biggest venues. When they were on MTV's *TRL*, with "Fat Lip" reaching number one, they weren't playing shows this big and selling this many tickets. The fact that I'm part of that and I helped rebuild that is amazing. I'm not angry about it at all. Yeah, to be honest, I don't want it to end—I wanna keep it going because it's too good. So that's gonna be hard to find again in other projects and other things because this is something that's pretty fucking rare.

I feel optimistic about the future and potential collaborations with each other. I don't see this as done forever because of the fact that we're such good friends and there's no drama. I remember Mötley Crüe; I was at their final show in 2015 in LA, and they didn't hang out after the show or even fist-bump each other before they went onstage because they were not speaking to each other. So when it was done, it was done, and they were fine with it. Then years later, they mended their issues and became friends again.

This ending is really good. It's the end of something for now, as hard as it is. I was the new guy replacing such a charismatic member. It's a great, respectable way to go out. So no, there was no "Fuck you, I'm mad at you." I was upset, of course, but it's not like we just got a call simply saying the band was done and that was it. It's not like we released a record without any promotion or fan service—that would've been a different story. That's certainly not the case here. We're handling it in the most respectable, admirable way possible.

Our first real show on the final tour was in Korea, and then we went to Malaysia, Indonesia, China, and all over Japan... I feel like Japan hit us all the hardest. It's a place we all love so much; it's been so special to us. We headlined a festival in Tokyo, and everyone was very quiet backstage after that show. I think that's when the reality hit: *We're not coming back to Japan anymore...*

During one of the shows in Japan, the AC was just blasting onstage, right onto Deryck, and it fucked up his voice. The next day, we did soundcheck, and it just wasn't 100 percent. He needed to let it recover for two days to avoid further damage, so we had to cancel the show in Nagoya. The fans were all queued up outside the venue, and we thought, "OK, we have to do something for these fans to say goodbye since we have to cancel this final show in Nagoya."

So we did a meet-and-greet. We went to the front of the line, and everyone could just walk alongside us, so we could fist-bump them, give hugs, whatever. It was one of the most devastating things I've ever done in my life. These fans looked us in the eye, and they're fucking crying because they were getting to meet us but they're saying goodbye at the same time. So we felt we were doing something good, but it was really hard emotionally. It took about an hour to meet everyone in line. Afterward, we went back to the hotel and everyone just went their own ways quietly. We did not meet for dinner, we didn't talk. It was fucking heavy, like we let the fans down, and then seeing the looks on their faces up close made it even harder.

After Asia, America was the second tour, spanning ten weeks divided into two legs. We did *Good Morning America*. I mean, the bucket list stuff we experienced on this tour cycle had been insane! So many firsts, so many holy-shit moments. We played Red Rocks for the first time and *that* was sold out—the biggest show of the band's American touring history. The biggest crowd, the most amazing show, the most beautiful show... There's just been so many moments, and my whole thing is trying to be present onstage and taking a moment to be grateful and reflect on what's happening while it's happening.

The European Tour was the biggest we've ever done. I think Paris truly embodied the beginning of the end. I had no idea how big it was until people started lighting their cell phones, showing just how far back and vast the limited-view seating was. It was the biggest headlining show the band's ever done, and hearing a fucking stadium roar like that sounded like a movie soundtrack. We were doing arenas the whole tour, 7,000 to 10,000 a night. To suddenly go into a stadium of 42,000? We're all fatigued. You know, we've been on the road for the whole year. It's the last show of the European Tour. We had to double our production to fill a stadium. Our entire team is there from all over the world—management to record execs. And just to add more fuel to the chaos, we've got a huge movie studio camera shoot happening, with cranes flying over the audience and robotics all over the stage. This thing is being saved forever, audio and video, like a film.

I had my family there, which was the first time I had my entire family in Europe with me to experience this. The emotions, everything... were just at a different level. Paris is one of our biggest markets ever, and it was the final European show.

It kinda hit me when we did our circle-up before we were about to hit the stage. Our guitar tech Tom (aka "Pocket Burger") was giving us a pump-up, which is always funny and comical. This time, however, his tone got serious and he was genuinely complementary to the band. I saw my family standing off in the distance, and I was about to lose it before even walking to the stage because it all just came full circle at that moment in every way. I got onstage, did the show, which was like just rocket fuel—amazing. The band played great. The crowd was insane.

But right before our last song, "In Too Deep," Deryck thanked the crowd, and that's when I definitely got emotional. Before we took the stage, the promoter presented us with plaques commemorating 42,000 tickets sold. And for the first time, I saw the whole band get really emotional. I knew how much that meant to them because the first time they went to France (before I was in the band), the record label, all the industry people told them, "This kind of music is never gonna work in France. You guys are never gonna be big here." It was all this negative stuff. And the band has stayed with the same promoter from day one. Paris is Sum 41's biggest market in the world; 42,000 tickets sold, a year in advance. The plaques took it to another level because I knew how much it meant to the guys.

When we played our last show in Los Angeles in the fall, it was the biggest headlining LA show of our career. We were about to hit the stage when our entire management team says, "Team meeting, now!" We're like, "We're about to take the stage. Why does the entire management company want to have a meeting *right now*?"

So they pull us into a room backstage, and they've got a laptop open with our entire team from Canada on Zoom. They read us an official letter from the Junos announcing that Sum 41 is being inducted into the Canadian Music Hall of Fame, and we are going to close the entire 2025 Juno Award show. We ran out just buzzing like you could never imagine. What rocket fuel to take onstage!

Fast-forward to our final Canadian tour, which was the largest Canadian tour we've ever done, headlining arenas. It was really incredible, and it served as the ultimate tour finale. We capped it off with two sold-out nights in Toronto—the band's hometown—in an NHL hockey arena to 20,000 people each night. The energy in the room was incredible, beyond emotional, a crazed roller-coaster ride to end this.

The thing that got me was I had my wife and kids there. My sister told me she was coming out solo and she was going to meet me in my hotel room. There's a knock on the door, and I can hear my sister yell "I'm here!" I open the door and my mother's there. My mother doesn't have a passport. She's never traveled outside of America. She doesn't enjoy traveling; she'll come to California to see me and that's about it. Somehow, she got a rushed passport just to be able to attend.

All our parents were there. All our kids were there. We couldn't do the two shows back-to-back because it was hockey season, so we did the first Toronto show, then a day off, then finally the last show. On that day off is when my wife, kids, mother, and sister were there. I booked a School of Rock workshop because I'd never done one in Canada. There are two schools in the area, and this is the coolest part: The venue we did it at, Metalworks, was the recording studio where Sum 41 made their first recordings. It's still in business! Wow! I did my workshop there with my family by my side.

I almost broke down multiple times onstage during the final show, knowing that my family was there plus all the emotions of saying goodbye, the final show. My sons and Tom Thacker's son went onstage and announced Gob (Tom's long-running band that opened the tour). They were so pro at it; these kids got the arena going nuts! Then my boys joined me onstage and tossed drumsticks out into the crowd. Just a really beautiful finale.

But wait! Even *that* wasn't the end. The next day we find out that the city of Ajax, where the band is from, has renamed the street where the dudes went to school and started Sum 41. Falby Court is now also known as Sum 41 Way. We went to the ceremony and they gave us a key to the city (which they had to create because it had never been done before in Ajax!). So we had this entire day with our family, team, and fans. It was just a beautiful finale to it all.

Oh, and the street sign's already been stolen… And replaced…

What did I tell you about our fans?

18
THE FUTURE IS IN/ON TIME

It's something I've literally battled with. I've worked my entire career to get to this level. It was a dream that has finally happened now, and there were some nights on this tour where I'd wonder, *am I ever gonna do this again*? *Am I ever going to get to play these packed rooms again and feel this roar and this energy*?

Then I would just quickly remind myself, *it always works out. If this is what you want to do, you're going to continue to do this.* But then I begin to think, "OK, I can get into another big band that's playing arenas. But if they don't generate this response—because I'm spoiled and used to performing in arenas with people going fucking mental—am I gonna be bummed out to be in an arena without that response when people are just looking at me? There's been so much of this roller coaster; I thought this might be the first summer that I don't go to Europe and play all these incredible festivals. And that's my favorite thing to look forward to every year…

Then I get an email from Electric Callboy, who are headlining all these festivals. They get the same response as Sum and they're playing arenas.

Before I got the call from them, I had seen that Guns N' Roses just got a new drummer. Iron Maiden, Primus… just *massive* bands. I was thinking, "Man, a lot of big gigs just got filled. Is this gonna be a really tough thing to land? Is it gonna take me a couple of years to find my footing?" All of that worry vanished when I got the call from these guys. How perfect is this: One band ends, an opportunity becomes available, literally right away to pick right back up again. It's an amazing theme throughout my life.

My wife even summed it up. She's like, "You're off the tour cycle now. You just *did* a big tour cycle. There'll be a lull now, and it'll pick back up again." That was her perspective. And it was good for me to hear that because I haven't been off a tour cycle for a minute here! And the good news is the tour dates I've seen so far with these guys, they're not like Sum 41 where you're out five weeks at a time with a short break and back out. It's a lot more tame, more manageable, which is very good for me and my family.

So fingers crossed that everything goes well. This is the new chapter of my life here. Yeah, I'm gonna have to really dig deep and work hard this summer on the festival run to truly earn my spot in the band. I love that challenge. I love the hard work that's going to come with it. I'm ready. It's like we're dating: How do we live together on a bus? How does the energy show up onstage? And if all is good, you know you're in. It's like "go prove yourself again."

Every new band is a new marriage. You could have 20,000 fucking Grammys, but if you don't mesh well personality-wise with other musicians, it's over. That's actually happened: There have been huge drummers who are bigger than a band or filled in for a band, and the band just didn't give a shit that he was an award-winning this or that. It just didn't jell personality-wise. I understand that side of it, especially when you've had the same drummer for the past 10 to 14 years. It's got to work musically and personally because it's a marriage. It's just got to be right, and I respect the process. There's just a lot that goes into it. I don't see it as me coming in there and being like, "I have all these accolades and you praise me and I'm the fucking king." I don't look at it that way.

Also, these guys are German, and Germans don't bullshit. They don't do the LA "Hey buddy" thing and tell you what you want to hear. I literally got offstage with them after the first festival gig we did, and they were straight-up with me: "Hey, this show was great, thank you. But here are a couple of things that we noticed," and they got right into it. There was no bullshit, which I actually respect. I respect the process, especially when it could lead to something bigger long-term for my career. Maybe it's just a challenge I'm putting on myself that keeps me motivated and inspired, I don't really know. It's just the way I'm programmed, and you know, it's all good.

To "Sum" up this final tour, I've got an emotional hangover. It's been emotionally, mentally, and physically exhausting in the best ways. And I feel like now that the Band-Aid's been ripped off and I have something so incredible, let's go! It's really exciting. Nerves and all the feels for the right reasons.

I say this every night from the stage during workshops. Mainly because I always get asked this, and that I think whatever you want to do, this applies to anything in life. Whatever you want to do in life, just do it, and don't stop until it happens. It's that simple. If you want to be a dentist, go be a dentist and be the best dentist you can be and learn everything you have to learn and *don't stop learning*. It's just that simple. That's why I do these workshops, just to tell the kids that I knew from five years old that this is what I wanted to do. And I'm still on that path. I continue to work at it, to learn, to study. That's the formula. Ask anybody who's gotten to where they are. Just ask, "How'd you get here?" They'll say, "Because this is what

I wanted to do. And I made sure it happened and I haven't stopped." That's just the key to it: Stay in that path, stay in that lane. That's *your* vision. I'm 100 percent proof of that.

Somebody asked me, "What would you do if you couldn't play drums any longer?" I paused: I don't even know. I don't have a response for that. It's like immediately I go into, "Well, there's a drummer that lost his foot, another lost his arm. And they play in bands now. How do we make it work? Like, can we do it in a wheelchair?" [*Laughs.*] I've seen crazy shit, so I don't know. I think I would somehow try to figure it out.

I never had a Plan B because… *I didn't want one*. I remember being in a fucking barber shop, and the guy was like, "Hey man, so obviously you can't do this drumming shit forever. Just know that if you ever want to be a barber, I got a chair for you here." In my mind, I'm like, *fuck you. Barber? What the fuck are you talking about?* Go tell that to Mick Fleetwood or Kenny Aronoff or Tommy Aldridge.

I can do this for the rest of my life.

ACKNOWLEDGMENTS

Thank You:
Lauren, Brixton, and Riot. It's a dream to be a husband and father to you! I love you endlessly! Hi Blaze and RIP Ripper!

Jason Pettigrew: Thank you for taking this journey with me!

My loving Mother and Sister for everything!
Dad: I hope you found your peace and I love you!
Mom and Dad Baird for being the absolute best! Poppa and Nonny for being the greatest grandparents and mentors! Uncle Dave (for taking me on my first tour), Jason Poirier, Godfather Uncle Charlie, my amazing DeFeis and Baird families!

David Frangioni, *Modern Drummer*, and Hal Leonard for believing in this and being my badass partner!

My brilliant team: Adam LaRue, Jeff Gandel, Gary Adelman, Dayna, Becky and Kerri-Ann @ BPM, Geoff Meal and Wasserman, Sound Talent Group, Miriam and Melissa @ Hisp4Hisp, Dr. Lee, John and Ayla @ Ascot.

Thank you, Dave Shapiro, for being such a supporter and great friend! Rest easy brother!

My Sum 41 and Electric Callboy brothers! You guys are truly the best brothers I could ask for!

Massive Love To: Shepard Fairey, Laird Hamilton, Gabby Reece, Kevin Lyman, Adrian Young, Gary Numan, Tommy Lee, Deryck Whibley, Dhani Harrison, Mike Ciprari, and Stacey Ryan. Thank you for being part of this book and such an important part of my life and story!

Thank you, Justin Imamura and family! Thanks for always being my rock and brother! #Bambino

Cheers to: School of Rock (all the amazing students, teachers, and owners), Rob Price, Alex Knagg, and SPTS

Coaches: Paul Dituro, Amy Shenk, Lenny Wiersma, PJ Nestler, Glenn Holmes, Mark Roberts, and XPT.

Dom Famularo, Drummers Collective NYC, Dave Elitch, LIDC, Chris Nary, Ron Laffitte, Jens Goedde, Shawn Dailey, Ben Davis, Charlie Weinmann, Eli James, John Meyers, Dajoe Berlei, Christian Ripkens, Tank, Crizzly, Josh Dun, Chester Bennington and family, Nikki Sixx, Robert Long, Ivan Copeland, Mike Shinoda, Anthony Bourdain, Scott Weiland, Chris Cornell, Liz Vegas, Viggy Vignola, Gabriel, PAPP, Sawicki, Alts, Terry and Gil, Bush Fam, Ryan Shuck, Matt Cranford, Mötley Crüe, SDC, Linkin Park, Krewella, Kayzo, theStart, Julien-K, The Zoo, The Used, Leto Bros, Deftones, grandson, The Offspring, Bert Kreischer, Curtis Douglas, Craymak, Danny Deleon, Jason Boucher, Dave Zonshine, DJ Aero, Brooks Wackerman, Stephen Perkins, Dan Estrin, Jimmy lovine, Ryan O'Donnell, DJ Lethal, Jamie Rise, Byron McCackin, Bert McCracken, Rise Records, Hopeless Records, Warcon Records, Scott Zant, Mike Green, Sum & EC Crews, Marko DeSantis, Create Music, Raymond Wei, John Asher, Lee Levin, Jauz and Bite This!, all the incredible artists that collaborated on my solo music, Drumeo, Sweetwater, AltPress, The Punk Rock Museum, LTTC, Steve Van Doren, Mitch Whitaker, Peter Dericks, Dan Kerby, Scott Helwig, John Lou and Studio 606, Drumtek, NY Giants, Dustin Hinz, The Rock and Roll Hall of Fame, Canadian Music Hall of Fame, Junos, Chase McCue and Hard Rock, Premier Collectibles, Craig Hollander, Darin Olien, John Germinario, John Reese, Sean Akhavan, Carl Stubner, Brad Fuhrman, Larry Tull, Gabe Van, Ray Volpe, Virtual Riot, Grabbitz, Jay Weinberg, Chris Qualls, Emo Nite, Lisa Johnson, Anthony Duty, Federica Burelli, Blake Primes, EastWest Studios, Howard Benson, Jonas Brothers, Good Day LA, Eric Fuller, and Forbes.

My incredible sponsors and support team:
SJC Drums, Steven Slate, Laird Superfood, 805, Primal Kitchen, Vans, Obey, Organixx, Plunge, Zildjian, Remo, Ahead, Roland, DW, Lowboy Beaters, Rock Locks, SE Mics, Vision Ears, UE, SKVI, Sleeved Washers, Snare Weight, and Cympad.

Thank you for reading this! Thank you to the amazing fans around the world for being part of this journey!
Much luv!
—FZ

Jason Pettigrew appreciates the grace, expertise, and effervescence of Frank Zummo, Adam LaRue, Ben Davis, The Blakes, DX Ferris, Annie Zaleski, Michelle Arevalo/ BiggHaus Ltd., and Hannah Aitchison.

Thank you for buying physical media.

PHOTO CREDITS

Front Cover photo: Christian Ripkens

Back Cover Photo: Dajoe Berlei

Alternative Press Awards backstage with Adrian Young & Josh Dun (2017-Cleveland, OH) Photo credit: Lizzy Gonzalez

Street Drum Corps in Bahrain on Military Tour (2014-Middle East) Photo credit: Zummo Archive

Bezerk performance with Tommy Lee & USC Drumline for Guitar Center Drum Off (2010-Los Angeles) Photo Credit: Rukes

Backstage warmup with coach Glenn Holmes (When We Were Young Festival, 2023-Las Vegas) Photo credit: Gentle Giant Digital

First show with Electric Callboy @ Good Things Festival (2024-Melbourne, Australia)
Photo credit: Christian Ripkens

Last time seeing Chester Bennington (2017-Backstage in Amsterdam) Photo credit: Blake Primes

Chester Bennington Celebration Show Finale (2017-Hollywood Bowl, Los Angeles) Photo credit: Linkin Park

Street Drum Corps with Chris Cornell (2008-Backstage on Projekt Revolution Tour) Photo credit: Zummo Archive

Crüefest 2 Finale (2009-East Coast America) Photo credit: Seraina Mars

My sister & I with our Father Frank Zummo Sr. (1980s) Photo credit: Zummo Family Archive

Sum 41 Final Show (2025-Toronto, Canada) Photo credit: Bradley Corman

Sum 41 Final Show Soundcheck with my Wife, Sons, Sister & Mother (2025-Toronto, Canada) Photo credit: Zummo Family Archive

First recording session with Sum 41 (2015-Hollywood) Photo credit: Sum 41

Baby Zummo on my father's 1976 Ludwig Drumkit (1980) Photo credit: Zummo Family Archive

Good Morning America with Sum 41 (2024-New York City) Photo credit: Zummo Archive

Great Wall of China with Mike Ciprari (2018) Photo credit: Zummo Archive

My first-born son Brixton (2016) Photo credit: Danielle Spires

With Jason Pettigrew & School of Rock Workshop at House of Vans Chicago (2023) Photo credit: Zummo Archive

Sum 41 induction into the Canadian Music Hall of Fame at the Junos (2025-Vancouver, Canada) Photo credit: Junos

Final Sum 41 Show with my sons Riot & Brixton (2025-Toronto, Canada) Photo credit: Crusty Media

Krewella live in Tokyo, Japan (2015) Photo credit: Zummo Archive

In Kauai with Gabby Reece & Laird Hamilton (2020) Photo credit: Zummo Archive

Backstage during Street Drum Corps Vegas Residency with Stephen Perkins, Adrian Young & Tommy Lee (2013) Photo credit: Erik Kabik

High School Marching Band (1990s-Half Hollow Hills East, NY) Photo credit: Zummo Family Archive

High School era in my parents basement (1990s-New York) Photo credit: Zummo Family Archive

My sister and I with our Mother (Early 1980s) Photo credit: Zummo Family Archive

Nike Marathon with Josh Dun (2018-Los Angeles) Photo credit: Zummo Archive

My Nonny & I (1978-New York) Photo credit: Zummo Family Archive

In Jerusalem with Gary Numan (2014) Photo credit: Zummo Archive

With Shepard Fairey at Obey studios Los Angeles (2018) Photo credit: Gentle Giant Digital

Reading & Leeds Festival with Mike Shinoda (2018-UK) Photo by: Federica Burelli

Red Rocks Colorado (2024-Sum 41 Final tour and biggest sold out headline US show) Photo credit: Blake Primes

My second-born son Riot (2018) Photo by: Gentle Giant Digital

Street Drum Corps at Vans Warped Tour San Francisco with Bert McCracken (2005) Photo by: Mike Watt

School of Rock Workshop (2025-Phoenix, AZ) Photo by: Lisa Johnson

First show with Sum 41 at Alternative Press Music Awards with DMC (2015-Cleveland, OH) Photo credit: Alt Press

The Drumheads have landed on Earth! (2022) Photo credit: Faive Shots

The Zoo, my East Coast cover band outta High School (1996) Photo credit: The Zoo

Backstage with Aimee Echo & Adrian Young. First show with theStart and Adrian was my sub! (2004-Chain Reaction, Anaheim, CA) Photo credit: Zummo Archive

First night in Toronto on Final Sum 41 tour (2025) Photo by: Blake Primes

Drumming at the bottom of Laird Hamilton's pool for my "E.O.T.E." music video (2020-Malibu, CA) Photo credit: Raymond Wei

Vans performance with Steve Van Doren & Mike Ciprari (2018) Photo credit: Gentle Giant Digital

Sum 41 Vans Warped Tour. My first-borns' first concert (2016-East Coast USA) Photo by: Lisa Johnson

Our Wedding Day with Reverend Dhani Harrison (2014-Newport Beach, CA) Photo by: Sylvie Cogranne

My Wedding Day with my Poppa Frederic DeFeis (2014) Photo by: Sylvie Cogranne

Elementary School jamming in my parents' basement (early 1980s-Brentwood, NY) Photo credit: Zummo Family Archive

With Anthony Bourdain (2017-Boston) Photo credit: Zummo Archive

Riding Tommy Lee's 360 Coaster with Lauren in Vegas! (2011) Photo credit: Tommy Lee

Vans TV appearance with Kevin Lyman, Steve Caballero & Steve Van Doren (2021) Photo credit: Zummo Archive

With Scott Weiland (2013-Reno, NV) Photo credit: Zummo Archive

Mini Street Drum Corps Zummo (1978) Photo credit: Zummo Family Archive

Coachella festival with Kayzo & special guests grandson, Yungblud, Alex Gaskarth & Tommy Lee (2019) Photo by: Ty Barch

Zummo family, Venezia, Italia (2024) Photo credit: Zummo Family Archive